PICTURE BOOKS

Integrated Teaching of Reading, Writing, Listening, Speaking, Viewing, and Thinking

JOYCE ARMSTRONG CARROLL

Illustrated by Leann Mullineaux

Jackdaws Series No. 1

1991
TEACHER IDEAS PRESS
A Division of
Libraries Unlimited, Inc.
Englewood, Colorado

I dedicate this series to my mother, Edwina, and to the memory of my father, Edwin, who together provided me not only with my first books but with the jackdaws by which I remember them still.

Copyright © 1991 Libraries Unlimited, Inc.
All Rights Reserved
Printed in the United States of America

No part of this publication may be reproduced, stored in a retrieval system, or transmitted, in any form or by any means, electronic, mechanical, photocopying, recording, or otherwise, without the prior written permission of the publisher. An exception is made for individual library media specialists and teachers who may make copies of activity sheets for classroom use, in-service programs, or other educational programs in a single school.

TEACHER IDEAS PRESS
A Division of
Libraries Unlimited, Inc.
P.O. Box 3988
Englewood, CO 80155-3988

Library of Congress Cataloging-in-Publication Data

Carroll, Joyce Armstrong, 1947-
    Picture books : integrated teaching of reading, writing,
listening, speaking, viewing, and thinking / Joyce Armstrong Carroll
; illustrated by Leann Mullineaux.
    64 p. 22x28 cm. -- (Jackdaws series ; no. 1)
    Includes bibliographical references.
    ISBN 0-87287-965-8
    1. Picture books for children--United States--Educational aspects.
I. Title. II. Series.
LB1044.9.P49C37 1991
371.3'2--dc20   91-19084
                                                                                  CIP

INTRODUCTION

In the May 1990 issue of *The Reading Teacher*, I happened upon the word *jackdaw*. I recalled that jackdaws are related to crows and wondered how the authors pulled jackdaws into an article on working with parents. As I read, I learned that Fredericks and Rasinski broaden the definition of *jackdaws* to "artifact collections related to a particular book," proposing that "after reading a book at home parents and children can be encouraged to make or find artifacts related to the book" (p. 693).

I thought about jackdaws, those mischievous and curious birds that love to carry away and conceal small bright objects that attract their attention, just as children enjoy having a memento of a favorite story. For the past several years I have been teaching others to generate, make, find, and use artifacts intrinsic to literature. When I read this article I knew that my interpretation of jackdaws, which would include the artifact, the concept, and the activity, would become the focus of this book.

While working with teachers to refine my jackdaws, I found that integrating writing, speaking, viewing, and thinking was easily accomplished through reading books and that teachers enjoyed calling the related activities and artifacts "jackdaws." As I worked with children in a variety of school settings, I found that adolescents as well as preschoolers enjoyed the activities and keepsakes inspired by a picture or storybook.

On the following pages I share many jackdaws. Because it was difficult at times to designate an exact grade level, I have given a range of levels for most activities. Both adults and children enjoy hearing and seeing a beautifully illustrated picture book or a Shel Silverstein poem. Topics such as characterization, dialogue, or metaphor are often easily taught through a short storybook. However, a novel by Robert Cormier would appeal primarily to adolescents and adults.

As you select your jackdaws, consider what will be appropriate for your participants, adapt the activities, and add your ideas to suit the needs of your students. Determine if students have allergies before serving food. You will find that as you share these books and activities, you and your students carry away many treasures, just like the curious jackdaw.

ACKNOWLEDGMENTS

Nothing happens in a vacuum in education. All of us work in tandem, we lead, we follow, we collaborate—above all, we share. While I have written this book to share ideas with teachers, librarians, parents, and others who read to young people and write with young people, I would be remiss if I did not credit those who helped make this series happen.

Some shared specific ideas, nuggets of pedagogy that turned into what you see on these pages. Some folks cornered me to share a great book they just discovered. Some shared information about books, books about books, articles, reviews, journals, and clippings. You were indispensable.

Some teachers shared their enthusiasm, their joy, their quiet working of daily miracles in their classrooms. Some tried a jackdaw and then sent the writings of the students. Bookstore owners and managers from one end of Texas to the other helped me search for the best books to include in this series. Thank you for your generous spirit.

And, of course, there were the librarians. I have always said they are our best friends, ever eager to find what we need. I have no reason to change that notion now. The teachers and trainers in the New Jersey Writing Project in Texas are especially appreciated for all their support and verve. I am also deeply grateful to all the people at Libraries Unlimited, especially David Loertscher, senior acquisitions editor, for believing in *Jackdaws* and Suzanne Barchers, my editor, for her assistance.

Finally to Eddie, my patient husband, worker of computers, fixer of things gone wrong, reader, listener, critic, and friend, you deserve the roundest applause of all.

Jackdaw 1

SPIDERS

Title: *The Very Busy Spider.* Philomel Books, 1984.

Author: Eric Carle

Grade level: Pre-K—2

Jackdaw: "Spiders" made out of Oreo™ cookies and licorice strips.

Summary: Through this multisensory book, children see and feel the very busy spider spinning her web as various farmyard animals try to distract her.

READING/WRITING CONNECTIONS

1. Begin with a spider story and then invite children to contribute other spider stories.
2. After reading the title and author, turn to the title page and run your hand over the spider's thread as you explain what makes this book special.
3. Stress the rhythmic pattern of the words and allow the children to see and feel the web as it grows.
4. Introduce the words *insect* and *arachnid*.
5. Talk about the two biggest differences between the two: the number of legs each has and their body parts. (Insects have six legs and three main body parts; arachnids have eight legs and two main body parts.)
6. Let students play detective by counting the number of legs on the creatures on the covers of *The Very Busy Spider, The Grouchy Ladybug,* and *The Very Hungry Caterpillar,* all Eric Carle books.
7. Make an arachnid, first demonstrating how to twist a cookie into two parts. Pull the licorice into eight pieces, then press the pieces into the cream of one side of the cookie. Replace the second part of the cookie on top.
8. Conclude with writing on themes such as "the last spider I saw," "spiders I have loved," "the messiest spider," or other spider stories. Share the stories in the class.

—EXTENSIONS—

VOCABULARY/SPELLING

bug	insect	silky	thread	neigh	bleated
spider	arachnid	spinning	grunted	crowed	owl

LIBRARY CONNECTIONS

1. Choral reading: Reread the book with the children participating in a choral response of *"The spider didn't answer. She was very busy spinning her web."*
2. Parts of a book: Show the title page again and discuss title, author, and publisher.
3. Corpus of work by an author: Check *An Author a Month (for Pennies)* by Sharron McElmeel for biographical information on Eric Carle. Gather other books by Carle (see list that follows), discussing how each is special and how each relates to science. Help children learn where to find Carle's books in the library.

JACKDAW 1—Copyright 1991 Teacher Ideas Press, a division of Libraries Unlimited, Inc., P.O. Box 3988, Englewood, CO 80155-3988

The Grouchy Ladybug
The Honeybee and the Robber
A House for a Hermit Crab
The Mixed-Up Chameleon
1, 2, 3 to the Zoo
Papa, Please Get the Moon for Me
The Tiny Seed
The Very Busy Spider
The Very Hungry Caterpillar

4. Find other famous spiders and webs in literature, such as in *Little Miss Muffet* (Offen), *Anansi the Spider* (McDermott), and E. B. White's *Charlotte's Web*.
5. Create a whole-class story (on chart paper) using Carle's pattern. Invite children to think of other animals who could talk to the spider, or use Anansi and jungle animals for a new twist.

SCIENCE CONNECTIONS

1. In the science section of the library, help children find books on insects and arachnids, such as Janet Craig's *Amazing World of Spiders*, so they can study the pictures.
2. The body parts of insects and arachnids: Distribute large sheets of butcher paper. On one side, children draw and label an insect's three body parts: head, middle (*thorax*), abdomen. On the other side, they draw and label an arachnid's two body parts: front (*cephalothorax*), or "head-chest," and back, or abdomen.
3. Check Carol and John Butzow's *Science through Children's Literature* for more ideas.
4. The webs of arachnids: Find a spider web outside. Carefully spray it with silver paint. Place black construction paper behind the web so it adheres. Bring it into the class to share with children.
5. Divide children into clusters. Give each cluster a set of plastic insects and arachnids that each group can separate into the two categories by applying the characteristics they have learned about each.

ART CONNECTIONS

1. Designing webs: Distribute pieces of black construction paper and white chalk. On the chalkboard or on posters, draw the five different types of spider webs (see list that follows) and label each. Children choose one to draw and label.
   - *Tangled web.* This is just a jumble of threads. Common house spiders usually make these webs in corners of walls or ceilings. Cobwebs are just ordinary spider webs that have collected dust.
   - *Triangle web.* This is usually made between branches of trees. It looks like a triangle.
   - *Bowl-and-doily web.* This looks like a bowl sitting on a doily. These are sometimes found around bushes.
   - *Dome web.* This uniquely shaped web looks like a dome and sometimes sits on or near the ground.
   - *Orb web.* This is the web spun by the very busy spider. It is large, round, and intricate.
2. Giving webs dimension: After the webs have been designed, use squeeze bottles of dimensional paint to retrace the web and give it the same dimensionality as the web in Eric Carle's book.

MUSIC CONNECTIONS

Everyone sings "Eensy Weensy Spider."

PUBLISHING

Place *The Very Busy Spider* in a prominent place. Invite children to create a display by surrounding the book with their webs and their writings about spiders. Join different elements of the display together with string or wool in imitation of a huge web.

Jackdaw 2 — HEALTHY HONEY TREATS

Title: *Brown Bear, Brown Bear, What Do You See?* Henry Holt, 1983.

Author: Bill Martin, Jr.

Grade level: Pre-K—2

Jackdaw: A healthy honey treat (see Science Connections) or a gummy bear.

Summary: On page after page, children see a variety of colorful animals and one mother looking at them.

READING/WRITING CONNECTIONS

1. Read the title and author. Show the basic parts of the book: cover, dust jacket, spine, pages.
2. Read the book and share the pictures, while inviting children to talk about what they see.
3. Reread the book and invite children to participate in a rhythmic reading of each page.
4. Have children imitate the sounds and movements appropriate to each animal.
5. Show a stuffed bear. Make up and tell its story. Invite children to share stories about their favorite bears.
6. Distribute gummy bears and invite children to write about their favorite bears.

—EXTENSIONS—

VOCABULARY/SPELLING:

brown	red	green
black	yellow	purple
gold	blue	white

LIBRARY CONNECTIONS

1. Research: Read and look at bear books, such as *The Little Polar Bear* series by Hans de Beer and nonfiction books about bears.
2. Corpus of work by an author, coauthor, or illustrator: Check *An Author a Month (for Pennies)* by Sharron McElmeel for more information on the author and additional ideas for this book. Show other books by Martin and explain the concept of a coauthor by discussing Martin's coauthor John Archambault. Explore the similarities and differences among books.
3. Discuss the artwork of Ted Rand. Compare and contrast Rand's artwork to that of Eric Carle (see Jackdaw 1). Compare the artwork of James Endicott in *Listen to the Rain* to that of Rand and Carle.

   Barn Dance
   The Ghost-Eye Tree
   Here Are My Hands
   Knots on a Counting Rope
   Up and Down on the Merry-Go-Round
   White Dynamite and the Curly Kidd

4. Literary appreciation: Create a book and bear corner. Display Martin and Archambault's books along with other bear favorites, including the classic *The Story of the Three Bears* or *Goldilocks and the Three Bears* (usually attributed to Robert Southey). Others might include

---

JACKDAW 2—Copyright 1991 Teacher Ideas Press, a division of Libraries Unlimited, Inc., P.O. Box 3988, Englewood, CO 80155-3988

A Bear Called Paddington by Michael Bond and its sequels; A. A. Milne's *Winnie the Pooh* and *The House at Pooh Corner*; Marjorie Flack's *Ask Mr. Bear*; and Else Minarik's *Little Bear*. Add bear calendars and posters. Invite children to bring in their stuffed bears and arrange them around the books.

5. Focus on bears by showing other books about bears:
   - Marta Koci's *Sarah's Bear* tells the adventures of a teddy bear.
   - Brinton Turkle's *Deep in the Forest*, wordlessly shows a switch on "Goldilocks."
   - Marjorie Weinman Sharmat's bear in *I'm Terrific* learns a valuable lesson.
   - David McPhail's *The Bear's Toothache* solves a big bear's problem.
   - David McPhail's *Fix-It* tells of replacing television with books for Emma.
   - David McPhail's *First Flight* tells about a teddy bear's first airplane flight.
   - Frank Asch's *Skyfire* explains what Bear does when he first sees a rainbow.
   - Bernard Waber's *Ira Sleeps Over* proves that even big kids love teddy bears.
   - Jane Hissey's *Old Bear* tells how Old Bear's friends rescue him.

SCIENCE CONNECTIONS

1. Hibernation: Cover a refrigerator box with brown papier-mâché to look like a cave. Children may "hibernate" as they read their chosen bear books or write or draw about bears.
2. Healthy honey: Make healthy honey treats by mixing honey and peanut butter. Put teaspoonsful of the mixture in tiny cups. Give each child a sesame stick and let them eat honey like bears.

SOCIAL STUDIES CONNECTIONS

1. Bear's habitats: Locate on a map places where bears live, such as wilderness areas and national parks.
2. Map-making: Let children draw freehand maps and then have them identify places where they think bears would live by pasting on bear stickers or stamping the areas with a bear stamp.

DRAMA CONNECTIONS

Rhythmic activity. Gather children in a circle. All bend over at the waist as they recite, "Brown Bear, Brown Bear, what do you see?" A child, designated as first, stands up straight and responds by calling up another bear he or she has "researched." For example, "I see a polar bear looking at me." All bend again, this time asking, "Polar Bear, Polar Bear, what do you see?" The next child responds and so on around the circle. Repeats, colors, numbers, and fantasy bears are acceptable.

ART CONNECTIONS

1. Bear-bag name places: Cut a brown shopping bag down the fold at each corner to the bottom. Draw a bear's head in one wide side section, a body in the section that was the bottom of the bag, legs in the other wide side section, and arms in the narrow side flaps. Have students write their names across the bear's chest. Girls put a red paper bow on the bear's head; boys at the bear's neck.
2. Decorated bear folders: Have children decorate folders to hold all their bear work.

PUBLISHING

Each child's bear sits in his or her chair for Parents Open House, holding the folder containing all the child's work in its lap.

JACKDAW 2—Copyright 1991 Teacher Ideas Press, a division of Libraries Unlimited, Inc., P.O. Box 3988, Englewood, CO 80155-3988

Jackdaw 3

POTTERY SHARDS

Title: *When the Clay Sings.* Aladdin Books, 1972. (Caldecott Honor Book, ALA Notable Book)

Author: Byrd Baylor; illustrated by Tom Bahti

Grade level: All levels

Jackdaw: Pottery shards (buy cheap pots to break, or obtain from a potter or the art department).

Summary: This book, rich in design and language, leads all readers to recognize "that every piece of clay is a piece of someone's life" by looking at the designs of prehistoric American Southwest pottery, as discovered by contemporary American Indian children. Some find shards and listen to the voices; some find pieces that fit together to tell stories; some find whole bowls that beg for dramatic play.

READING/WRITING CONNECTIONS

1. Either in or outside the classroom, strategically place bits of pottery.
2. Read aloud, stopping at places such as, "They say that every piece of clay is a piece of someone's life," or "They even say it has its own small voice and sings in its own way." Explore what students think those sentences mean.
3. Invite students to embark on a pottery hunt. When they find a piece of clay, they are to hold it, study it, listen to its voice, and figure out its creator's life. Discuss their ideas.
4. Have students write about and share what they discovered in their clay.

—EXTENSIONS—

VOCABULARY/SPELLING:

ancient	bowl	wide-eyed	whisper
Indian	pretend	deerskin	feather
blanket	language	speckled	costumes
thousand	polishing	cliffhouse	flute
whirlwinds	skinny	turtles	medicine
fierce	wrestling	mountain	canyon
lizards	antelope	lion	wildcats

LIBRARY CONNECTIONS

1. Awards: Discuss the Caldecott and the American Library Association awards. Older students can research these awards: criteria for awarding, year they began, and some books that have received these awards.
2. Corpus of work by an author: Gather other books by Baylor. Look at the artwork by Tom Bahti and Peter Parnall and discuss the style of each.

Amigo
The Best Town in the World
The Desert Is Theirs
Hawk, I'm Your Brother
If You Are a Hunter of Fossils

JACKDAW 3—Copyright 1991 Teacher Ideas Press, a division of Libraries Unlimited, Inc., P.O. Box 3988, Englewood, CO 80155-3988

Everybody Needs a Rock
Feet!
Guess Who My Favorite Person Is

I'm in Charge of Celebrations
The Way to Start a Day

3. Research: Folklore is sometimes called the "mirror of people." It includes songs, festivals, dance, rituals, stories, and art. Students can research the folklore of the Anasazi, Mogollon, Hohokam, and Mimbres cultures by using reference materials, including atlases, encyclopedias, almanacs, and other reference books.

SOCIAL STUDIES CONNECTIONS

1. Study the geography and topography of the American Southwest by making "baker's clay" relief maps of this area. To make baker's clay, measure and mix 1 cup flour, ½ cup salt, and 2 tsp. cream of tartar. Add 1 cup water, 2 Tbsp. oil, 2 tsp. vanilla extract, and 8-15 drops of food coloring, if desired. Heat. Stir over high heat about 3 minutes or until the "dough" clumps into one huge ball and "cleans" the pan's sides. Cool. Knead out any lumps. Store in airtight containers for future use or sculpt into relief maps immediately.

2. Study the American Southwest Indians: Have students examine the art designs on the pottery of the Anasazi, Mogollan, Hohokam, and Mimbres cultures of Arizona, New Mexico, Utah, and Colorado. Compare and contrast with designs found in the caves of France and Spain. Use books such as Keith Brandt's *Indian Crafts* and *Indian Homes* for younger children. All levels may create a paper border for the classroom of designs discovered during their research.

3. Discuss the word *prehistoric* and introduce the word *archaeological*. Discuss how archaeologists deduce things about ancient peoples from artifacts, just as students did by examining pottery shards.

ART CONNECTIONS

1. Field trip: Take a field trip to a museum that features Native American art. Use the book *Visiting the Art Museum* by Laurene Krasny Brown and Marc Brown to prepare students for the trip; pages 31 to 32, "Tips for Enjoying an Art Museum," are particularly good.

2. Creating an exhibit: Set up an area where students can display the shards they received as jackdaws. Using their imaginations and what they discovered doing research, have students write a card to accompany each shard, giving an approximate date and cultural source. Younger students might imagine where the shard came from, give a name to its place of origin, and provide a date.

3. Creating Indian designs: Distribute large pieces of sepia-colored paper. Have students work together in groups to make a mural with Indian designs, following Bahti as a model.

MUSIC CONNECTIONS

Writing a chant. Share a chant such as "A Chant Out of Doors" by Marguerite Wilkinson (in *Bluestone*). Ask students to join in a second reading.

Divide students into groups to research, write, and perform a group chant. They may also model Paul Fleischman's *I Am Phoenix: Poems for Two Voices* or *Joyful Noise: Poems for Two Voices* to create and perform chants for two voices or groups.

PUBLISHING

Small groups may create a part of a class book on chants, using as a model *Dancing Teepees: Poems of American Indian Youth* (poems selected by Virginia Driving Hawk Sneve, with art by Stephen Gammell).

JACKDAW 3—Copyright 1991 Teacher Ideas Press, a division of Libraries Unlimited, Inc., P.O. Box 3988, Englewood, CO 80155-3988

Jackdaw 4

BALLOONS

Title: *The Blue Balloon.* Little, Brown, 1989.
Author: Mike Inkpen
Grade level: 1-3
Jackdaw: Balloons or balloon stickers.
Summary: Through pages that open in various ways, the reader "sees" a little boy blow up a wonderful balloon that never bursts, despite being stretched, squeezed, squashed, whacked, run over, and let fly.

READING/WRITING CONNECTIONS

1. Give students a balloon apiece and invite them to imitate the actions of the narrator as you read along. (Have extra balloons on hand, as real balloons *will* burst.)
2. Lead students through a mapping of the book. Begin with the book's title and brainstorm words.
3. Have children write and illustrate about their own balloons.

Making a Balloon Book

Show a model of an eight-page book and demonstrate how to make an eight-page *Prewriting Balloon Book*:

- Fold an 8-inch by 11½-inch piece of paper in half, short end to short end, and crease.
- Fold back one side halfway and crease; fold back the other side halfway and crease. (If opened fully, the paper would be creased in four long rectangles).
- Keeping the paper folded, fold it short end to short end and crease. (If opened fully, the paper would have eight rectangles).
- Unfold the last fold and allow the sides to flip down (the center fold will look like a tent peak; the paper can stand by itself on a desk or table).
- Rip carefully or cut down from the peak of the tent where the center folds meet. Cut only down to the next fold.
- Pick the paper up with one hand on either side of the cut. Fold down so the cut is across the top. You will need to recrease one fold.
- Fold into the shape of a book.

Prewriting in the Books

1. Invite students to use their eight-page books for prewriting a story about balloons, using the following pattern:
   - Page 1 or cover—Write your name. You may return to title it or add a design later.
   - Page 2—Write adjectives that describe *balloons.*
   - Page 3—Write verbs (action words) that tell what balloons do or what can be done with balloons.
   - Page 4—Write adverbs that apply to how balloons do what they do.
   - Page 5—Pretend you are talking to a friend about your balloon. What would you say? Write down that dialogue.

JACKDAW 4—Copyright 1991 Teacher Ideas Press, a division of Libraries Unlimited, Inc., P.O. Box 3988, Englewood, CO 80155-3988

- Page 5—Pretend you are talking to a friend about your balloon. What would you say? Write down that dialogue.
- Page 6—Write what your balloon is like or unlike.
- Page 7—Write what your balloon might say if it could talk.
- Page 8—List some ideas for a story about your balloon.

2. Talk about each page first to encourage oral responses as examples. Using the prewriting books for ideas, have students write stories about their balloons in another eight-page book.

—EXTENSIONS—

VOCABULARY/SPELLING

soggy	shiny	squeaky	whacked
ordinary	balloon	squashed	indestructible

LIBRARY CONNECTIONS

1. Research: Encourage children to find books with unusual construction and share their discoveries with classmates.
   - Mitsumasa Anno's *Anno's Peekaboo* has movable paper hands in front of faces.
   - Eric Carle's *Papa, Please Get the Moon for Me* has pages that fold out.
   - Eric Carle's *The Secret Birthday Message* has a code which cut pages uncover.
   - Harriet Ziefert and Mavis Smith's *In a Scary Old House* has fold-out pages.
   - Tony Bradman's *Look Out, He's Behind You!* is a lift-the-flap book.
2. The making of books: Study Aliki's *How a Book Is Made*.

SCIENCE CONNECTIONS

1. Air power: Show how to lift a book without touching it. Put a balloon on a table so its opening hangs over the table edge. Put a book on top of the balloon. Raise the book by blowing up the balloon. Discuss how air under pressure can move heavy objects.
2. Static electricity: Show how to stick a balloon on a wall. Take a blown-up balloon and rub it against something woollen or against hair. Put the balloon against a wall and let it stick. Discuss how the balloon became charged.

SOCIAL STUDIES CONNECTIONS

1. Research on balloons:
   - Find out why and when people send balloons as gifts.
   - Look up Charles Goodyear and then report to the class what he discovered.
   - Look up the history of balloons to find when they were first used and who used them.
2. Sources of rubber: Read about how rubber is extracted from trees and plants. Locate on a map and read about lands that grow rubber trees and plants.

ART/LANGUAGE ARTS CONNECTIONS

1. Making "rubber maps": Draw a map of India, Malay, or another rubber-producing place. Affix tiny rubber objects such as erasers and rubber bands to the map and list the many uses of rubber in the map's margins.
2. Make another eight-page book. Using the dictionary, find at least six words that have the word *rubber* in them (for example: *rubberneck*). Illustrate one word on each page of the book and write something funny for each.

PUBLISHING

Display the writings, drawings, maps, and books around an old tire. Include nonfiction books about rubber. Call the display "The Rubber Works."

JACKDAW 4—Copyright 1991 Teacher Ideas Press, a division of Libraries Unlimited, Inc., P.O. Box 3988, Englewood, CO 80155-3988

Jackdaw 5

ACCORDION BOOKS

Title: *The Important Book.* Harper & Row, 1949.
Author: Margaret Wise Brown
Grade level: All levels
Jackdaw: An accordion book.
Summary: Through the cadence of language, this book stimulates the senses and awareness of what is important about everyday, mundane things, such as a spoon, a daisy, a shoe, as well as about self.

READING/WRITING CONNECTIONS

1. After introducing the book, read about the cricket, calling attention to the parenthetical statement "(you tell me)." Explain the cadence of the book and invite children to join in as you read.
2. Together compose an "important" page. Use the inside cover and title-page suggestion of *glass* as the starter.
3. Compose a page aloud for each of the other objects on the inside cover and title page.
4. Choose an object in the room as the subject of a composition using the cadence "Wise uses."
5. Students are now ready to compose on their own. Ask them to think of something important they could describe using the cadence "Wise uses."
6. Show students how to make an accordion book:
   - Fold a piece of paper in half.
   - Fold one side back halfway.
   - Fold the other side back halfway. The accordion book will thus have a cover and seven long, narrow pages (counting both the front and back of the paper).
7. On the cover, students write "*The important thing about _____ is that _____.*" On pages one through six, they write a different description, each not quite as important as the one on the cover. On panel seven, they simply write the word *B U T*.
8. Because the cover and page eight of an accordion book are the same, the book becomes recursive, emphasizing the **important thing.**

—EXTENSIONS—

VOCABULARY/SPELLING

cadence   shovel   hollow   ticklish   crystal   tender

LIBRARY CONNECTIONS

1. Main idea/main plot and secondary ideas and subplots: Students apply this cadence to pieces of literature by using an accordion book to extract the main idea or main theme and the subthemes or subplots. For example, high-school students studying *Macbeth* might work up an accordion book like this:
   - Cover: *The important thing about **Macbeth** is that the play is about ambition.*
   - Page one: *It is true that the play also deals with guilt.*
   - Page two: *It also tells about delusion.*

JACKDAW 5—Copyright 1991 Teacher Ideas Press, a division of Libraries Unlimited, Inc., P.O. Box 3988, Englewood, CO 80155-3988

- Page three: *It shows the many facets of despair.*
- Page four: *It includes weakness and conflict.*
- Page five: *It emphasizes torment and pathos.*
- Page six: *Still, it contains elements of courage, loyalty, and imagination.*
- Page seven: **B U T**
- [Page eight is the cover: Same as "Cover" above.]

    Students may then elaborate on each page's statements.

2. Corpus of work by an author: Gather other books by Brown. Display in the Author's Corner.

    The City Noisy Book
    David's Little Indian
    The Dead Bird
    Goodnight Moon
    The Little Fireman
    The Little Island (written under her pseudonym Golden MacDonald)
    The Runaway Bunny

SCIENCE CONNECTIONS

Making a main hypothesis: Students follow the same cadence working with an experiment. (See *More Science Secrets* by Judith Conaway and Renzo Barto.)

- Cover: *The important thing that will make this experiment on growing plants work is the sun.*
- Page one: *It is true that you need six clear plastic cups.*
- Page two: *It is also true that you need paper towels.*
- Page three: *It requires seeds.*
- Page four: *It needs masking tape.*
- Page five: *It needs a pen.*
- Page six: *It needs a paper clip.*
- Page seven: **B U T**
- [Page eight is the cover: Same as "Cover" above.]

SOCIAL STUDIES CONNECTIONS

Supporting a main idea: Students follow the cadence to support a main idea, changing BUT to **SO**.

- Cover: *The important thing about George Washington was that everything during his eight-year term of office was a "first."*
- Page one: *He was the first president of the United States.*
- Page two: *He was married to the first First Lady.*
- Page three: *He authorized the first U.S. Census.*
- Page four: *Under Washington, we had the first U.S. Mint.*
- Page five: *He convened the first session of the Supreme Court.*
- Page six: *He announced the first official Thanksgiving.*
- Page seven: **SO**
- [Page eight is the cover: Same as "Cover" above.]

PUBLISHING

Display students' "important" accordion books around Margaret Wise Brown's *The Important Book*. Juxtapose appropriate objects and other books with their books.

JACKDAW 5—Copyright 1991 Teacher Ideas Press, a division of Libraries Unlimited, Inc., P.O. Box 3988, Englewood, CO 80155-3988

Jackdaw 6 — CLOTH ALPHABET LETTERS

Title: *Chicka Chicka Boom Boom.* Simon & Schuster Books for Young Readers, 1989.

Author: Bill Martin, Jr., and John Archambault

Grade level: Pre-K—2

Jackdaw: A letter of the alphabet made from felt.

Summary: Personified letters of the alphabet climb a coconut tree accompanied by a rhyming, rhythmic chant.

READING/WRITING CONNECTIONS

1. Introduce the book and invite predictions about the book.
2. Read the book in a rhythmic, chanting way.
3. Reread the book and ask children to join in.
4. Distribute individual letters of the alphabet made of felt to individual children.
5. Explain that when "their" letter is read from the book, they are to put that letter on a coconut tree which you have made out of felt, glued to a larger piece of felt, and laid on the floor.
6. Read the first part of the book again as children place their letters on the tree. When you come to "The whole alphabet up the—Oh, no!," mix up all the letters by shaking the "tree."
7. As you read the second part, children retrieve their letters. Reread as appropriate.
8. Allow children to tape their letters onto something in the room that begins with that letter (for example, C on the closet, B on a book).

—EXTENSIONS—

VOCABULARY/SPELLING

coconut   alphabet   tangled   knotted   looped   stooped

LIBRARY CONNECTIONS

1. Different alphabet books: Show children several alphabet books, such as:
   Action Alphabet by Marth Neumeier and Byron Glaser
   A Is for ANGRY by Sandra Boynton
   C Is for Curious by Woodleigh Hubbard
   The Z Was Zapped by Chris Van Allsburg

   Compare and contrast these books with *Chicka*, noting similarities and differences.
2. Corpus of work by an author (see Jackdaw 2).

SCIENCE CONNECTIONS

1. Coconut trees: Show children pictures of coconut trees. Point out the texture of the bark and the characteristic shapes of palm leaves. Compare the leaves of the coconut tree to the leaves of other trees, as found in another ABC book called *A B Cedar: An Alphabet of Trees* by George Ella Lyon. Using Lyon's book as a model, have children create a page about the coconut tree.
2. Coconuts:
   - Bring in several coconuts. Let children feel their texture, look at their shapes, and tell what they look like.

JACKDAW 6—Copyright 1991 Teacher Ideas Press, a division of Libraries Unlimited, Inc., P.O. Box 3988, Englewood, CO 80155-3988

- Drain the liquid from one as the children watch. (You will probably need a hammer and ice pick to punch through the "eyes" to drain the coconut.) This is "coconut milk." Other products from coconuts are coconut cream and coconut oil.
- Give children a tiny taste of coconut. Talk about what it tastes like and discuss things made from coconut.

3. The coconut crab: Tell children about the coconut crab, a large land crab that lives in the South Pacific and eats coconuts. Children can draw pictures of what they think this crab might look like.

SOCIAL STUDIES CONNECTIONS

Where coconut trees grow:
- Find the South Pacific on a map of the world or on a globe. Call attention to the islands in that area and teach children what makes a body of land an island.
- Generally talk about that area: its climate, its people, its culture.
- Have students find out all the products that come from coconut trees.

ART CONNECTIONS

1. Making coconut trees: Give children white paper, a piece of brown burlap, and two different colors of green felt for making coconut trees. (Posters of *Chicka Chicka Boom Boom* are available through Silver Burdett & Ginn. These make a wonderful display, and children can use them as a visual model.)
2. Creating leaf collages: Give each child a large green piece of construction paper cut in the shape of a palm leaf to use as the base for a collage of other leaves they find.

PUBLISHING

Children make their own ABC books, either alone or in groups, following ideas gleaned from books they have read. Advanced students may vary their books by adding a bit of logical thinking and using as their model *Q Is for Duck* by Mary Elting and Michael Folsom.

Jackdaw 7 — FRUITS AND VEGETABLES

Title: *Eating the Alphabet.* Harcourt Brace Jovanovich, 1989.

Author: Lois Ehlert

Grade level: Pre-K—2

Jackdaw: Miniature plastic fruits or vegetables or real fruits and vegetables (as described in Science Connection 3).

Summary: This book provides a journey through the alphabet by way of the names and colorful pictures of fruits and vegetables.

READING/WRITING CONNECTIONS

1. Ask children to identify the fruits and vegetables on the cover and invite predictions.
2. Show the title page and discuss the funny face pictured there.
3. Read the book, inviting responses to the letters and pictures.
4. Distribute the jackdaws and have children identify them.
5. Ask children to write a page about their fruits or vegetables.

—EXTENSIONS—

VOCABULARY/SPELLING

title   introduction   glossary   fruit   vegetable

LIBRARY CONNECTIONS

1. The introduction: Read the book's introduction. Generally talk about introductions and then have children introduce themselves to the whole class and to a single classmate. Talk about why people and books need introductions.
2. The glossary: Show the book's glossary. Explain the function of a glossary and read some interesting excerpts.
3. Corpus of work by an author: Gather other books by Ehlert and create a Lois Ehlert Author's Corner. Help children learn how to find Ehlert's books in the library.

   Color Zoo   *Growing Vegetable Soup*
   Feathers for Lunch   *Planting a Rainbow*
   Fisheyes: A Book You Can Count On

   You may want to include books illustrated by Lois Ehlert, such as *Chicka Chicka Boom Boom*.

4. Research: On the copyright page, Ehlert quotes Anthelme Brillat-Savarin's saying, "Tell me what you eat, and I will tell you what you are." In the reference section of the library, show children how to find books of quotations and share some of the interesting quotations found therein.

JACKDAW 7—Copyright 1991 Teacher Ideas Press, a division of Libraries Unlimited, Inc., P.O. Box 3988, Englewood, CO 80155-3988

SCIENCE CONNECTIONS

1. Learning about fruits and vegetables: Use this book to reinforce letter recognition while teaching the identity of various fruits and vegetables.
2. Classifying fruits and vegetables: Divide children into groups. Give each group stylized, colored-paper replicas of the fruits and vegetables in the glossary and have them paste picture under one of the headings on a chart labeled "FRUITS," "VEGETABLES," and "FRUITS AND VEGETABLES." They may check the book as they work.
3. Preparing fruits and vegetables: Under careful supervision, allow children to prepare some fruits and vegetables to be eaten. They may cut carrots, apples, bananas, celery, and tomatoes. An alternative is to bring fruits and vegetables that may be prepared without cutting, such as sectioned oranges, tangerines, or grapefruits; stemmed cherries or grapes; leaves of lettuce or watercress; or pieces of cauliflower or broccoli. If your budget permits, give each child a berry of some kind, and try to get something unusual to share with the children, such as star fruit, ugli fruit, or jicama.

SOCIAL STUDIES CONNECTIONS

1. Map making: Have children choose a country that produces fruits or vegetables. After they have drawn a map of that country, they can research and draw in the fruits and vegetables that come from there.
2. Christopher Columbus: Help children trace the route Columbus took when he brought corn to Europe from the West Indies.

ART CONNECTIONS

Fruit and vegetable faces: Using the model on the title page, make faces using stylized cut-out or drawn fruits and vegetables.

MUSIC CONNECTIONS

Sing and skip to "Oats, Peas, and Beans," from *Go In and Out the Window* (music arranged and edited by Dan Fox).

PUBLISHING

After children write stories about their fruit and vegetable faces, display the art and the stories emerging from a large cornucopia. Intersperse with artificial fruits and vegetables.

JACKDAW 7—Copyright 1991 Teacher Ideas Press, a division of Libraries Unlimited, Inc., P.O. Box 3988, Englewood, CO 80155-3988

Jackdaw 8

CLAY POTS

Title: *The Pottery Place.* Harcourt Brace Jovanovich, 1987.

Author: Gail Gibbons

Grade level: 3-8

Jackdaw: A clay pot.

Summary: Explains the making of a pot by following a potter throughout the process. The book also has a two-page map spread that encapsulates the history and geography of pottery-making.

READING/WRITING CONNECTIONS

1. While showing the book's inside front and back covers and endpapers, talk about the texture and look of those pages.
2. Follow the delivery truck and invite predictions about what might be delivered.
3. Before reading, discuss the book's title page and dedication.
4. Give students time to study the two-page map spread that chronicles the history and geography of pottery.
5. Distribute ready-to-use air-dry clay to each student. Using the last page of the book, which tells how to make three kinds of pots, let each student choose whether to make a pinch pot, a coil pot, or a slab pot.
6. After making their pots, let students write a "How To" paper, giving explicit directions on how to make that type of pot. Or have students write group or individual stories on the theme, "what I learned about making a pot." Share pots and papers in small groups.

—EXTENSIONS—

VOCABULARY/SPELLING

wheel head   shaft   kick wheel   cones   flywheel   kiln

LIBRARY CONNECTIONS

1. Research:
   - Using the card catalog, locate information on pottery, pottery-making, and/or the history of pottery.
   - Locate any filmstrips or films on pottery, pottery-making, and/or the history of pottery.
   - Find the art section of the library and allow students to choose books that would help them create interesting designs or patterns to paint on their pots.
2. Context clues: Using context clues and pictures from the book, ask students to write definitions for all the pottery terms listed in the Vocabulary section. Check definitions first with the whole class and then with definitions in a dictionary or an encyclopedia.

JACKDAW 8—Copyright 1991 Teacher Ideas Press, a division of Libraries Unlimited, Inc., P.O. Box 3988, Englewood, CO 80155-3988

SOCIAL STUDIES CONNECTIONS

1. Find the locations of the pottery shown on the two-page map spread on a globe, on a map of the world, and in the atlas.
2. Research the cultures of the various people who created pottery as shown on the two-page map spread:

African potters	Grecian potters
American Indian potters	Iranian potters
Chinese potters	Japanese potters
Cretan potters	Mexican potters
Egyptian potters	Peruvian potters
English potters	Spanish potters

ART CONNECTIONS

1. Field trip: Visit a museum. Students may study the pottery exhibits to help them plan their own exhibits.
2. Pottery design: As students decorate their pots with appropriate designs, encourage them to refer to their research (see Library Connection 1).
3. Exhibiting pottery: Divide students into groups to create an exhibit of the students' pottery, including display plans, labels, and references to books.
4. Artist demonstration: Invite a local potter to show some pots he or she has made and to demonstrate the making of pottery. Include a question-and-answer period.

ECONOMICS AND MARKETING CONNECTIONS

1. Marketing research: Research the difference between pots made from molds and those made by hand.
2. Cost of materials: Research the costs of porcelain, red clay, ceramic ware, stoneware, and earthenware.
3. Pricing: Based on the information gathered, let students assess their own wares and perhaps even offer them for sale if a student store exists.

PUBLISHING

Create a Pottery Place in which each group can display charts, essays, or stories along with pottery made by the group.

JACKDAW 8—Copyright 1991 Teacher Ideas Press, a division of Libraries Unlimited, Inc., P.O. Box 3988, Englewood, CO 80155-3988

Jackdaw 9

SPECIAL ILLUSTRATIONS

Title: *Jambo Means Hello: A Swahili Alphabet Book.* Dial Books for Young Readers, 1974.

Author: Muriel Feelings; illustrated by Tom Feelings

Grade level: Pre-K—2

Jackdaw: Artwork using Tom Feelings's technique.

Summary: Muriel Feelings introduces children to the culture of East Africa through the alphabet, through Swahili words with their definitions and explanations, and through accompanying illustrations.

READING/WRITING CONNECTIONS

1. Begin a discussion of East African life and the book by talking about the title page and pointing out the title, author, and illustrator.
2. Read the dedication. Invite students to infer what it tells about the author.
3. Read the introduction. Make an overhead transparency of the map of Africa and point out places where Swahili is spoken.
4. Read through the book, showing the words and pictures. Stop after ones that particularly interest children, such as *heshima* (respect—the act of kneeling before an elder) or *shule* (school, which is usually held outdoors).
5. Explain that this book was designated a Caldecott Honor Book because of its art. (Show the medal on the cover, if possible.) Tell students that they will have the opportunity to do some artwork in Feelings's style.
6. After children copy the art technique (see Art Connections), ask them to write about the objects they painted. Display the coordinated artwork and writing.

—EXTENSIONS—

VOCABULARY/SPELLING
Africa   Swahili

LIBRARY CONNECTIONS

1. Awards: Talk about the many awards this book received, which are listed on its inside cover.
2. Caldecott Award: Examine the illustrations in this book. Show children some of Tom Feelings's illustrations for Maya Angelou's *Now Sheba Sings the Song* and Eloise Greenfield's *Daydreamers.*
3. Library awareness: Show children where they can find books on art and books on Africa.

JACKDAW 9—Copyright 1991 Teacher Ideas Press, a division of Libraries Unlimited, Inc., P.O. Box 3988, Englewood, CO 80155-3988

4. Introduce other books on Africa:

    Bringing the Rain to Kapiti Plain by Verna Aardema
    Darkness and the Butterfly by Ann Grifalconi
    Shaka: King of the Zulus by Diane Stanley and Peter Vennema
    The Village of Round and Square Houses by Ann Grifalconi

5. Share *Moja Means One: A Swahili Counting Book*, also by Muriel Feelings.
6. Choral speaking:
    - Use the riddle "The Elephant Carries a Great Big Trunk" found on page 110 in *Fun with Choral Speaking* by Rose Marie Anthony.
    - Use "*A Story, A Story* Rhythmic Activity" found on pages 175-76 in *Learning through Literature* by Carol Sue Kruise.

ART CONNECTIONS

1. To copy Feelings's art technique, use the following process:
    - Make a pencil sketch of something in the classroom.
    - Go over the pencil lines with black, water-based, fine-tip marker.
    - Paint white water tempera in any area that should be left light.
    - Lay a wet sheet of tissue paper over the whole drawing, allowing the colors to bleed for an interesting effect.

SOCIAL STUDIES CONNECTIONS

1. Reading maps, globes, and the atlas: Study the map presented in the book of the continent of Africa. Have children find Africa on a large map of the world, on the globe, and in an atlas.
2. Making maps: Let children draw the map of Africa on brown paper bags; then cut the maps out and label places where Swahili is spoken.

MATHEMATICS CONNECTIONS

Count the number of letters in our alphabet. Count the number of letters in the Swahili alphabet. Which one has more letters? How many more?

MUSIC CONNECTIONS

1. Drum and dance (*ngoma*): Let children beat a rhythm and dance to some familiar songs.
2. Stringed instruments (*zeze*) and xylophone: Ask children to bring in banjos, guitars, and xylophones to play.

PUBLISHING

Create a Swahili Day to feature all the artwork, books, musical instruments, and writing that pertains to the study of Africa.

JACKDAW 9—Copyright 1991 Teacher Ideas Press, a division of Libraries Unlimited, Inc., P.O. Box 3988, Englewood, CO 80155-3988

Jackdaw 10   POP-UP AND MOVABLE BOOKS

Title: *Leonardo da Vinci.* Viking Press, 1984.
Author: A. Provensen and M. Provensen
Grade level: 3-12
Jackdaw: Pop-up and/or movable books.
Summary: Through this three-dimensional, movable picture book, readers are introduced to the inventive and artistic genius of Leonardo da Vinci.

READING/WRITING CONNECTIONS
1. Introduce the book by showing a small stuffed bird (available from craft stores) or a picture of a bird and discussing the fascination with flight that has existed since people began watching birds and wondering what it would be like to fly.
2. Show the cover of the book, pointing out and discussing the design for a "flying machine." Talk about how each picture surrounding da Vinci's portrait tells of one facet of his genius.
3. Read the introduction from Giorgio Vasari's *Lives of the Artists.*
4. Invite the students to manipulate and discuss each page.
5. Divide students into groups of four to brainstorm names of people they have studied about whom they could do a pop-up and/or movable book. After library research, each group chooses one person. Each group member plans one page to research more thoroughly, write, and produce. Assign a deadline day on which projects must be completed and shared with the rest of the class.
6. Demonstrate how to make a simple pop-up book: On the fold of a file folder, measure a two-inch box, counting the fold as one side of the box. Cut the two lines perpendicular to the fold. Crease on the parallel line. Open the folder and push the cut box through, recreasing the fold so it forms an upright tent in the middle of the open folder. Pictures glued or stapled to that box will pop up when the folder is opened. Multiple boxes may be cut from one folder, and folders can be stapled together to form a book.
7. If some students want to make movable pages, they may study the da Vinci book. These are generally complicated and time-consuming and demand precision of measurement, so allow time to assemble the books.

—EXTENSIONS—

VOCABULARY/SPELLING

astronomer	architect	engineer	inventor
apprentice	bronze	ingenious	porous

LIBRARY CONNECTIONS
1. Have students use an atlas to find Italy and a gazetteer to find Florence.
2. Ask students to use an encyclopedia to find information about modern Florence and Florence during the fourteenth to sixteenth centuries. List the information under *Then* and *Now.*

JACKDAW 10—Copyright 1991 Teacher Ideas Press, a division of Libraries Unlimited, Inc., P.O. Box 3988, Englewood, CO 80155-3988

4. Invite students to begin notebooks formatted like da Vinci's jumbled, five-thousand-page notebook. They may include drawings of humans, animals, plants, flowers, trees, stars, geometric forms, words, formulae, any and all things of interest to them. Permit them to comb the library for books that stimulate their creativity and jot their findings in the notebooks. They may even try writing entries backwards and from right to left as da Vinci did.
5. Introduce etymological dictionaries and the *Oxford English Dictionary* for use in researching da Vinci.

SOCIAL STUDIES CONNECTIONS

1. Construct a dimensional map of Italy (see Jackdaw 3), using papier-mâché to show the topography of the country. Rivers may be placed with silver or blue ribbons. Place Florence on the Arno River.
2. Draw a genealogy chart for the Medici family.
3. Make an exhibit of the artistic and intellectual works of Florentines such as Dante, Boccaccio, Donatello, Raphael, and Michelangelo.

ART CONNECTIONS

1. Create a mural that represents da Vinci's life and accomplishments.
2. Research the Mona Lisa. After their research, students may write about what Madonna Elisabetta may have been thinking during the three years (1503-1506) da Vinci painted her portrait, or they may want to write a verbal portrait to match the Mona Lisa.

SCIENCE CONNECTIONS

1. Da Vinci was fascinated with simple machines, always applying their principles to create his inventions. Young children may read *Simple Machines* by Rae Bains to learn about the lever, wedge, wheel, screw, pulley, and inclined plane. Older students may study David Macaulay's *The Way Things Work*. Da Vinci also believed in experience as a scientific method; encourage students to test some of these simple machines by designing or producing their own.
2. Construct two mobiles, one showing the planets and the solar system before da Vinci, the other showing da Vinci's idea of the solar system.
3. Encourage students to become inventors like da Vinci. Consult and use the strategies in *Inventing, Inventions, and Inventors* by Jerry D. Flack.

MATHEMATICS CONNECTIONS

1. Let students design a parachute by mathematically scaling down the one described by da Vinci: "If a man have a tent made of linen, of which the apertures have all been stopped up, and it be twelve cubits across and twelve in depth, he will be able to throw himself down from any great height without sustaining any injury."
2. Younger students may make a top parachute (see *More Science Secrets* by Judith Conaway).

PUBLISHING

Hold a class Renaissance Fair. Consult chapter 11 in *Fanfares* by Jan Irving, or make a display of pop-up books.

JACKDAW 10—Copyright 1991 Teacher Ideas Press, a division of Libraries Unlimited, Inc., P.O. Box 3988, Englewood, CO 80155-3988

Jackdaw 11

DINOSAUR COOKIES

Title: *If Dinosaurs Were Alive Today.* Price Stern Sloan, 1988.

Author: Lisa Hilton and Sandra L. Kirkpatrick

Grade level: 1-5

Jackdaw: Dinosaur cookies.

Summary: Through creative illustrations, the names of the dinosaurs, and a clever sentence about each of fourteen dinosaurs, readers learn facts about dinosaurs by imagining them alive today.

READING/WRITING CONNECTIONS

1. Show the cover of the book and invite students to explain why the illustration is funny. Then find and read that page in the book, explaining that the entire book is written that way.
2. Move through the book by first showing the picture, inviting responses, then giving the fact. (In many cases the students will predict the fact.)
3. Give students dinosaur cookies and invite them to write other facts and different sentences to go with the dinosaurs pictured on their cookies. (For example: If certain dinosaurs were alive today they would be called king; *rex* in *Tyrannosaurus rex* means "King.")

—EXTENSIONS—

VOCABULARY/SPELLING

Megalosaurus	Deinonychus	Iguanodon	Triceratops
Dimetrodons	Eryops	Stegosaurus	Tyrannosaurus rex
Lambeosaurus	Polacanthus	Protoceratops	Diplodocus
Psittacosaurus	Trachodon		

LIBRARY CONNECTIONS

1. Find the dinosaur section in the library. Share pictures and information about dinosaurs from various reference books, including books that give facts, such as Joyce Milton's *Dinosaur Days*.
2. Explain that some books have sequels. Share Carol Carrick's *Patrick's Dinosaurs* and its sequel *What Happened to Patrick's Dinosaurs?* Then introduce her latest, *Big Old Bones: A Dinosaur Tale*.
3. Read some of the riddles from Noelle Sterne's *Tyrannosaurus Wrecks: A Book of Dinosaur Riddles*. Invite the students to write and share some original riddles.
4. Show students dinosaur story books. Tell them enough about each book to intrigue them into reading the whole thing. (For example, Francis Mosley's *The Dinosaur Eggs* is about a lonely couple who find three eggs and hatch a dinosaur family.)

JACKDAW 11—Copyright 1991 Teacher Ideas Press, a division of Libraries Unlimited, Inc., P.O. Box 3988, Englewood, CO 80155-3988

Several books deal with finding and bringing dinosaurs home, among them Henry Schwartz's *How I Captured a Dinosaur*, Jane Thayer's *Quiet on Account of Dinosaur*, and William Joyce's *Dinosaur Bob and His Adventures with the Family Lazardo.*.

Other amusing dinosaur books include Dennis Nolan's *Dinosaur Dream*, Lorinda Bryan Cauley's *The Trouble with Tyrannosaurus Rex*, and Laurene Krasny Brown and Marc Brown's dinosaur guide books, *Dinosaurs Travel: A Guide for Families on the Go* and *Dinosaurs Divorce: A Guide for Changing Families*.

HEALTH CONNECTIONS

Use Marc Brown and Stephen Krensky's *Dinosaurs, Beware!* as a delightful safety guide. Invite children to create a dinosaur safety poster.

SCIENCE CONNECTIONS

Divide the class into groups and give each group some plastic dinosaurs to identify and classify. Do not give specific directions; let students discover or create categories according to size, weight, period of existence, etc.

ART CONNECTIONS

1. Finger puppets: Use Peter Seymour's *Baby Dino's Busy Day* to introduce finger puppets. Have students make dinosaur finger puppets so they can put on a puppet play. See *One-Person Puppet Plays* by Denise Anton Wright for more details.
2. Dioramas: Make shoe-box dioramas with dinosaurs.

MATHEMATICS CONNECTIONS

Use Nancy Blumenthal's *Count-A-Saurus* to reinforce counting and dinosaur names. The "Append-a-saurus" provides accurate and interesting information on each type of dinosaur. Students in the upper elementary grades can make original counting books of this sort for children at the primary level.

POETRY CONNECTIONS

Share poems such as "I Saw a Brontosaurus" in Jack Prelutsky's *Something BIG Has Been Here*, "Pachycephalosaurus" in *Sing a Song of Popcorn* (selected by Beatrice Schenk de Regniers), "If I Had a Brontosaurus" in Shel Silverstein's *Where the Sidewalk Ends*, or any of the poems Lee Bennett Hopkins selected in *Dinosaurs*. Have students write their own dinosaur poems and publish them in a class *Big Book of Dinosaur Poems*.

MUSIC CONNECTIONS

Play square-dance records and invite students to sing and dance the "Square Dance" from Jane Yolen's *Dinosaur Dances* as dinosaurs might. Play some disco records and invite students to move with "Disco Dino Dancing."

PUBLISHING

For Dinosaur Days, decorate the room with plants, hanging (sterilized) Spanish moss, and books. Display all the art, writing, and science projects completed during this unit.

Jackdaw 12

POSTCARDS

Title: *Stringbean's Trip to the Shining Sea.* Greenwillow Books, 1988.

Author: Vera B. Williams and Jennifer Williams

Grade level: 3-8

Jackdaw: A postcard.

Summary: Stringbean (Cesar) Coe and his brother Fred capture their trip to the Pacific Ocean in a series of postcards which they send to folks back home.

READING/WRITING CONNECTIONS

1. Begin by reading a postcard you have received. Model by telling how you felt when that postcard arrived and explaining why you felt that way.
2. Discuss if anyone ever received or sent a postcard.
3. Discuss the difference between postcards and letters. Discuss why we send postcards when we are traveling.
4. Introduce and read through the book, always inviting students to point out what they notice as different or interesting about the postcard pages (such as the stamps, the addresses, the messages, even the signatures). (This book may be read over two or three days so that details may be scrutinized and savored.)
5. Distribute blank postcards. Invite students to follow Stringbean's example by writing a message, making a stamp, addressing the postcard, and designing a front. (Refer to the sentence under the book's copyright notice, which tells what materials were used to create the postcards.) Share the postcards.

—EXTENSIONS—

VOCABULARY/SPELLING

| stringbean | shining | automotive | junkologist | propane stove | sod house |
| midwife | bison | trekked | phantom | pinto | trestle |

LIBRARY CONNECTIONS

1. Road atlas: Since Stringbean talks about a road atlas on his second postcard, show one to students and point out its features.
2. Road maps: Divide students into groups. Give each group a road map of the United States and have students use markers to plot out Stringbean's trip.
3. Extended reading to cover all grade levels: Encourage students to find other books that deal with trips and travel.
   - Ann Jonas, *The Trek.* While trekking to school, a child imagines jungles and deserts.
   - Dick Gackenbach, *With Love from Gran.* Gran sends presents from travels.

JACKDAW 12—Copyright 1991 Teacher Ideas Press, a division of Libraries Unlimited, Inc., P.O. Box 3988, Englewood, CO 80155-3988

- Chris Van Allsburg, *Ben's Dream*. Ben dreams he visits different places.
- Nigel Gray, *A Balloon for Grandad*. Sam's balloon travels to Egypt.
- Pat Brisson, *Kate Heads West*. Kate uses letters to describe her trip.
- Clayton Bess, *Tracks*. Blue and Monroe travel the railroad tracks.
- Jean Fritz, *Homesick: My Own Story*. Fritz describes life in China and America and the trip from Shanghai to San Francisco.
- Joan Lowery Nixon's *In the Face of Danger: Orphan Train Quartet* recounts the travels of children from the New York slums to homes in the West.
- Cynthia Voigt, *Homecoming* and *Dicey's Song*. Dicey takes James, Sammy, and Maybeth from the town where they were stranded to Gram's.
- Will Hobbs, *Changes in Latitudes*. A story begins during a family trip to Mexico.

SCIENCE CONNECTIONS

1. Bird research: Using encyclopedias and reference books on birds, take notes on the fourteen birds pictured and named on one of Stringbean's postcards.
2. Ocean study: Stringbean's Pacific Ocean postcard gives data about the ocean. Research other oceans and report some interesting facts about them.
3. Endangered species: Postcards refer to buffalo, seals, whales, and salmon. Discover why these species are endangered and research other endangered species.
4. Life spans of various species: Using Stringbean's postcard as a model, create a chart of the life spans of different living creatures.
5. The horned lizard: On one postcard Stringbean tells about the horned lizard. Do more research on this or other interesting lizards.

SOCIAL STUDIES CONNECTIONS

1. Prairie life: Compare Stringbean's experiences on the prairie to those in Laura Ingalls Wilder's books, in Patricia MacLachlan's *Sarah, Plain and Tall*, and in Carol Ryrie Brink's *Caddie Woodlawn*.
2. Ghost towns: Research ghost towns in the United States. Discuss what caused them to be deserted. Write a cause/effect paper on ghost towns or write a compare/contrast paper on a town before and after it became a ghost town.
3. Graveyards: Visit a graveyard as Stringbean did. What do the tombstones tell about the people or the history of the area?

MATHEMATICS CONNECTIONS

1. Metric units: Stringbean writes on one postcard "ONLY 300 MILES (THAT'S 482.7 KILOMETERS) TO THE PACIFIC OCEAN." Calculate where Stringbean was when he wrote that postcard. Calculate Stringbean's whole trip in kilometers. Calculate distances in miles and kilometers from one point to another (for example, from a student's house to school).
2. Reading maps and estimating miles: Plot several routes on a map. Then estimate the miles between sites, using rulers and the map's legend. Add the miles given on the map along the route you plotted. Compare the two numbers.

PUBLISHING

Plan a Welcome Home party for Stringbean. Decorate the room with maps and postcards. Rename and label refreshments after Stringbean's adventure: "Bison cookies," "cactus juice," "Jeloway dessert."

JACKDAW 12—Copyright 1991 Teacher Ideas Press, a division of Libraries Unlimited, Inc., P.O. Box 3988, Englewood, CO 80155-3988

Jackdaw 13

NAMED OBJECTS

Title: *Merry-Go-Round: A Book about Nouns.* Grosset & Dunlap, 1990.

Author: Ruth Heller

Grade level: All levels

Jackdaw: A "noun" (object) pulled out of a bag.

Summary: An aesthetically rhythmic study of nouns.

READING/WRITING CONNECTIONS

1. Hold up an object (a miniature merry-go-round would be ideal but not essential). Give its name. Then give its grammatical name—*noun*.
2. Ask each student to give the name of the object he or she has pulled from a bag. Reinforce repeatedly that the name of each object being held is a noun.
3. Use the title page to identify a thing (e.g., horse) and its classification (i.e., noun).
4. Read through the book and let students identify the nouns given on each page. When appropriate (given the grade level and knowledge of the students), have them apply the concepts covered in the book to their objects. For example, when discussing common and proper nouns, suggest that each student try to convert his or her common noun to a proper one (horse—Trigger).
5. Give students paper and colored markers. Let each create a page following Heller's model for the noun he or she has chosen.

—EXTENSIONS—

VOCABULARY/SPELLING

common nouns	proper nouns	abstract nouns	concrete nouns
compound nouns	collective nouns	singular nouns	plural nouns
plural compounds	possessive nouns	determiners	hyphenated

LIBRARY CONNECTIONS

1. Rhythmic reading: Reread the book, stopping at places that invite students to supply the rhyming word.
2. "Readers Theatre of Nouns": Using the objects they were given, students work in groups to create a readers theatre presentation, incorporating as many concepts about nouns as they can. See *Readers Theatre for Children* and *Readers Theatre for Young Adults* by Mildred Knight Laughlin and Kathy Howard Latrobe for directions on scripting techniques.
3. Corpus of work by an author: Help students find other books written or illustrated by Ruth Heller in the library.

JACKDAW 13—Copyright 1991 Teacher Ideas Press, a division of Libraries Unlimited, Inc., P.O. Box 3988, Englewood, CO 80155-3988

Animals Born Alive and Well
A Cache of Jewels and Other Collective Nouns
Chickens Aren't the Only Ones
The Egyptian Cinderella (text by Shirley Climo)
Kites Sail High: A Book about Verbs
Many Luscious Lollipops: A Book about Adjectives
Plants That Never Ever Bloom
The Reason for a Flower

SCIENCE CONNECTIONS

1. Nouns in science: Distribute large pieces of construction paper. Working in groups, students create a collage of "Nouns in Science." Do not give too many specifics: some may want to accompany words with pictures; others may want to relate their collages to a theme, such as "environment nouns." Challenge students to fill the paper with as many words as possible. See how many the entire class found.

2. Quick Wit: Test Your Brain Power: Divide students into groups of two and assign the partners to work up a list of ten nouns used in science that fit all the types Heller discusses, such as compound nouns, plural nouns, collective nouns, etc. Then have two groups face each other in a contest. One group gives a word from its list—for example, "fishes." The other group responds with something like, "*Fishes* is the plural form of *fish*," or "*Fish* is a singular noun; *fishes* is a plural noun."

ART CONNECTIONS

Noun plates:

- Take two paper plates of the same size. Using a dictionary, students list nouns around one plate like the numbers on the face of a clock. Designate categories. For example, have some students make "Proper Name" plates and other students make "Plural Compound" plates. These become the bottom plate.
- Cut a one-inch wedge in the other plate. Title and decorate this (top) plate in Heller's style. Affix the two plates with a brad or paper fastener so the top plate will rotate easily over the bottom plate.
- With a partner, students drill each other using each other's noun plates.

MUSIC CONNECTIONS

1. Noun Rap: Divide students into groups. Each group prepares a "rap"-style song or chant of Heller's book to share with the class.

2. Background music: Divide students into groups. Each group explores different kinds of music to use as background to a reading of Heller's book and explains its choices. Tape the chosen pieces and play during a reading of the book.

PUBLISHING

Display all work done on nouns using a merry-go-round motif.

Jackdaw 14

FACE FRAMES

Title: *I Can Blink.* Crown Publishers, 1985.

Author: Frank Asch

Grade level: Pre-K—1

Jackdaw: A page with a one-pound-coffee-can-size hole cut out of it.

Summary: Each page tells what a different animal does with its face. The hole invites children to provide the facial expressions. The last two pages work with self-esteem.

READING/WRITING CONNECTIONS

1. Tell children you intended to read them a book but something terrible happened. Show them the book. Put your hand through the hole and ask them to tell you what part is missing, presenting the missing part as a problem to be solved. (Someone always comes up with the idea of putting one's face in the hole.)
2. Read a page. Invite a child to read the page, following your model. Work through the entire book, rereading as necessary.
3. Distribute a blank page with a hole cut out of it for each child to write on. Accept all efforts and have each child read his or her page.

—EXTENSIONS—

VOCABULARY/SPELLING

| blink | owl | sniff | turtle | shake | squirrel |
| snake | monkey | scrunch | walrus | wiggle | rabbit |

LIBRARY CONNECTIONS

1. Corpus of work by an author:

    Bear Shadow *Popcorn*
    Happy Birthday, Moon *Sand Cake*
    I Can Roar *Skyfire*
    Moon Bear

    Gather these books together for a display. Help children learn where to find books by Asch in the library.

2. *I Can Roar*: Repeat the *I Can Blink* procedure, but this time have children mimic the sounds animals make.
3. Related books: Share with children other books that have something missing:
    - Carol Jones's *Old MacDonald Had a Farm* asks children to guess what animal comes next by looking through a peep hole.

JACKDAW 14—Copyright 1991 Teacher Ideas Press, a division of Libraries Unlimited, Inc., P.O. Box 3988, Englewood, CO 80155-3988

- Carol Jones's *This Old Man* asks readers to guess which object comes next by looking through a peep hole.
- Tana Hoban's *Look! Look! Look!* invites readers to guess about familiar things by looking through a peep square.
- Nancy Hellen's *Old MacDonald Had a Farm* reveals the farm animals to children through its board pages and die cuts.
- Leslie McGuire's *Nibbles Takes a Nibble* contains holes on each page.

SCIENCE CONNECTIONS

Habitats of animals: Three titles—*Be Quiet, Go Slowly* by Elva Robinson; *When All the World's Asleep* by Roach Van Allen; and *Peeking Out of a Tree* by Trena Allen—undergird the concepts covered in the Asch books. *Science Predictable Storybooks: A Teacher's Guide* by Roach Van Allen offers suggestions for activities.

ART CONNECTIONS

Let children make stick puppets of the different animals in the Frank Asch books (see Denise Anton Wright's *One-Person Puppet Plays*).

MUSIC CONNECTIONS

1. Sing-along with stick puppets: Students sing "Old MacDonald Had a Farm," adding verses to include each of the stick-puppet animals. When the class sings the verse for an animal, children work the appropriate puppets.
2. Discovering tempo: Play different tempos of music. Children reenact the movements of animals that go with that tempo. For example, you might play Beethoven's Fifth Symphony while children mimic lumbering bears.

PUBLISHING

I Can Be Anything ... I Can Be Me! display:
- Create a bulletin board in the form of a three-dimensional display. After covering a bulletin board with butcher paper (or paper from a newsprint roll), tear a tiny hole in the center of the paper. Peel back fifteen to twenty strips of paper outward from the center hole like spokes of a wheel, making a larger hole in the middle of the paper. The farther back the ribbons are torn, the larger the hole will be. The strips are each arched into a back loop and then taped down. The overall result will look like a flower with loops for petals.
- Put pictures of the class within the circle and the pages children made from the *I Can Blink* reading/writing activity outside the circle.
- Display all the unique books on a table in front of the class.

JACKDAW 14—Copyright 1991 Teacher Ideas Press, a division of Libraries Unlimited, Inc., P.O. Box 3988, Englewood, CO 80155-3988

Jackdaw 15

LEATHER STRIPS

Title: *Barmi: A Mediterranean City through the Ages.* Houghton Mifflin, 1990.

Author: Xavier Hernandez and Pilar Comes

Title: *The Sandal.* Viking Kestrel, 1989.

Author: Tony Bradman and Philippe Dupasquier

Grade level: 9-12

Jackdaw: A thin strip of leather.

Summary: Barmi is a fictional city, the history and evolution of which are traced through panoramic sketches and explanatory text.

In *The Sandal*, readers see both changes and connections between the past and the future through pictures, prose, and a sandal.

READING/WRITING CONNECTIONS

1. Begin by explaining that you have two books that are closely related. Show the covers of each and invite speculation and predictions.
2. Read *The Sandal*. Be sure to give students time to notice the little girl drop the sandal in the future.
3. Read *Barmi*. (You may want to take two days for these readings.) Give students ample time to investigate the drawings and to find places. Encourage them to look at these drawings more closely on their own time.
4. Distribute the strips of leather. Ask students to pretend they have found these "sandal straps," and invite them to write and then share their speculations about the time period in which their "finds" were lost.

—EXTENSIONS—

VOCABULARY/SPELLING

metropolitan	colonization	feudalism	syntheses
endeavor	humanistic	legionary	reconnaissance
cisterns	silos	forum	basilica
amphitheater	provincial	insulae	barbarian
garrison	ecclesiastic	theology	philosophy
ramparts	artisan	facade	opulence
mint	baroque	moat	bastions
citadels	barracks	quarantine	commercial
neo-classical	urban	infrastructure	slaughterhouse
sewage	residential	suburban	telecommunication

JACKDAW 15—Copyright 1991 Teacher Ideas Press, a division of Libraries Unlimited, Inc., P.O. Box 3988, Englewood, CO 80155-3988

LIBRARY CONNECTIONS

1. Library research: Divide students into groups of two. Each group researches information about the century assigned (use the centuries represented in the books). Each pair then presents the information in a manner appropriate to the way information was disseminated in that century. For example, those researching the fourth century B.C. might tell their information orally as a story, whereas the late twentieth-century group might provide theirs on a computer printout.

2. Time line: Groups of four students construct a time line of the development of the sites giving dates as well as centuries.

3. Where's Waldo in Barmi?: Using the book *Where's Waldo?* by Martin Handford, students working in groups reproduce one of the Barmi aerial drawings. For example, the "Commercial Expansion: Mid-Fifteenth Century" group might place Waldo in the main square, or an artisan's workshop, or in the university. Groups exchange their "centuries," including a "Where's Waldo?" checklist, with other groups.

SOCIAL STUDIES CONNECTIONS

1. Research: Choose one of the following topics mentioned in the fictional Barmi to research. Based on your findings, evaluate the accuracy of the story of Barmi.

The Mediterranean region	Punic War	Augustus Caesar
Hannibal	Byzantine Empire	Constantine
Charlemagne	The Franks	Gothic style
Plagues and epidemics	Renaissance	Monarchies
The Industrial Revolution	Opera	World War II

2. Cities: Research an ancient city (for example, Rome or Cairo). Build a model city out of plaster of paris.

SCIENCE CONNECTIONS

Research the scientific achievements of each of the centuries depicted in *Barmi*, from the discoveries of how to smelt and forge metals to the discovery of TNT.

ART CONNECTIONS

Show "The Edifice," the first segment in Saul Bass's film *Why Man Creates*. The edifice being constructed in this segment is a visual metaphor for the history of the civilization of man, and the segment itself is a cinematic version of *Barmi*. Use David A. Sohn's *Film: The Creative Eye* to help make a detailed analysis of the film.

PUBLISHING

Plan a Grand Fair in Celebration of the Ages of Humankind. Assign students a section of the library or classroom to decorate in the manner of their century and in which to exhibit all their research about that century. They may dress in the manner of their century, offer foods appropriate to their century, and display the art and play the music of their century.

Jackdaw 16

FEATHERS

Title: *Five Secrets in a Box.* E. P. Dutton, 1987.

Author: Catherine Brighton

Grade level: 3-5

Jackdaw: A feather (obtain at craft store).

Summary: Galileo's daughter Virginia finds a box with five objects inside that reveal the world to her.

READING/WRITING CONNECTIONS

1. Show the cover of the book. Ask if anyone can tell where the story takes place by the landmark they see through the window. Also ask if students can figure out the time period of the story and/or what it might be about.
2. Take out a box you have previously prepared containing a feather, a blue lens, a red lens (you could use red-tinted and blue-tinted transparencies), and two pieces of magnifying glass. Ask students to predict what the five secrets in the box might be. Set the unopened box aside after their predictions.
3. Read the book, giving ample time for students to notice all the details in both the full-page picture and the small picture accompanying the text. As you read, take each object in turn out of your box. Last, read the introductory information.
4. Give each child a feather. After explaining that the feather reminded Virginia of her father's work, invite students to think of objects that remind them of the work their mothers or fathers do. Have them write the names of those objects and why those objects remind them of what one of their parents does.
5. Students share in small groups by giving the name of an object and letting others see if they can guess the work associated with it. Then they read what they wrote about that object.

—EXTENSIONS—

VOCABULARY/SPELLING

landmark   instruments   oriole   fragment   falcon   rustle

LIBRARY CONNECTIONS

Dedication and acknowledgments:
- Invite students to brainstorm reasons why an author would dedicate a book to someone not living.
- Point out all the research and travel the author did to write this book. Ask the students to speculate on how traveling to Italy, visiting the Museum of the History of Science, and seeking the advice of the assistant curator of the museum helped the author.

JACKDAW 16—Copyright 1991 Teacher Ideas Press, a division of Libraries Unlimited, Inc., P.O. Box 3988, Englewood, CO 80155-3988

SOCIAL STUDIES CONNECTIONS

1. Italy: On a map of the world, have children find the country of Italy. Ask them what it looks like.
2. Pisa: On a map of Italy, have children find the city of Pisa, where Galileo was born and where he taught.
3. The Leaning Tower of Pisa: Show children the tower on the book's cover. Explain that it is considered a landmark. Show them Chris Van Allsburg's *Ben's Dream*, which also has a picture of this landmark.

SCIENCE CONNECTIONS

1. Classroom experiments: Divide the class into four groups. Rotate the groups so that each group works with one of the secrets from the box for about five minutes.
   - Bring magnifying glasses, telescopes, and/or binoculars to class. Give the students the opportunity to use them as Virginia did.
   - Use red-tinted glass or transparencies for students to observe what the change to a red color does to objects.
   - Repeat with blue-tinted glass or transparencies.
   - Have each student drop a feather and a pebble. Discuss what happens and why, reminding students that Galileo said both objects would fall at the same rate only if there were no air.
2. Galileo's discoveries: Using his astronomical telescope, Galileo discovered the four largest satellites of Jupiter and the stellar composition of the Milky Way. He also supported the Copernican system of heliocentric planetary motion. Students may do library research in teams on the following: the astronomical telescope, Jupiter's satellites, the Milky Way, Nicholas Corpernicus, and Claudius Ptolemy. Compile and share the research.

ART CONNECTIONS

Make a diorama out of a shoebox:
- Paint the inside back and sides dark blue or black.
- Make cardboard representations of each of the planets in the solar system.
- Suspend these, according to the Copernican system, from the roof of the shoe box.

Planets and the Solar System by Keith Brandt is one inexpensive but accurate and colorful resource.

MUSIC CONNECTIONS

Play *The Planets*, op. 32, by Gustav Holst (1874-1934). Students may draw each of the planets as they listen, or they may simply listen. Following the music, they may talk about what they imagine as the music changes to fit each planet. Speculate as to why there is no music for Earth or for Pluto.

PUBLISHING

Create a display of books and students' work around a large box labeled "Five Secrets in a Box."

Jackdaw 17

PARTY HATS

Title: *Surprise Party.* Grosset & Dunlap, 1990.
Author: David A. Carter
Grade level: Pre-K—2
Jackdaw: Silly party hats.
Summary: Colorful illustrations, fantastic flip-up flaps, and puzzling pop-outs take the reader through a guessing game of who is at Mr. and Mrs. Alligator's house.

READING/WRITING CONNECTIONS

1. Give each child a party hat to wear in preparation for the reading of the book. Before showing the book, ask the children about when they wear these kinds of silly hats. Talk about parties.
2. Show the book. Read the title and author and ask students to guess what kind of a party this book is about.
3. Read each page. Permit the children to open each window. Invite speculation based on the clues given behind each window.
4. When the reading is over, invite the children to make birthday cards with pop-out mouths that open to say "Happy Birthday" to the baby alligator:
   - Fold a standard-size piece of construction paper in half. Cut or rip a two-inch slit in the middle of the paper, perpendicular to the fold.
   - With the paper still folded, take one side of the cut at the fold and crease into a deep triangle. Do the same with the other side of the cut. (Your paper will look like a V-neck collar.)
   - Bend the triangles back to their original positions.
   - Make a tent with the construction paper with the center fold as the peak.
   - Gently push the two triangles through, recreasing them on the inside of the paper. (When you close the paper, you have a clean *V* on the outside. Inside, you have a moving beak.)
   - Draw an animal around the beak and then write the birthday message.

—EXTENSIONS—

VOCABULARY/SPELLING

slithery	sticky	fancy	feathers	beautiful	thirsty
fabulous	frosty	windows	claws	beaks	fingers

LIBRARY CONNECTIONS

1. Corpus of work by an author: Share Carter's *How Many Bugs in a Box?* (a pop-up counting book), *More Bugs in Boxes* (a pop-up book about color), and Peter Seymour's *What's in a Jungle?* (a lift-the-flap, pop-up book), which Carter illustrated.

2. Share other pop-up/pop-out, movable books:
   - Pelham and Foreman's *Worms Wiggle*, which is based upon lines from the poem.
   - "Jump or Jiggle" by Evelyn Beyer, from *Another Here and Now Story Book* by Lucy Sprague Mitchell.
   - Shapiro and Paris's *The House on Main Street*, a read-around pop-up book.
   - Moerbeek and Dijs's *When the Wild Pirates Go Sailing*, a pop-up adventure book.
   - Moerbeek and Dijs's *Hot Pursuit*, a forward-and-backward pop-up book.
   - Tripp's *The Bad Child's Pop-Up Book of Beasts* with verses by Hilaire Belloc.

SCIENCE CONNECTIONS

1. Jungle animals:
   - Talk about alligators. Ask children where alligators live.
   - Talk about other jungle animals.
   - Read B. G. Hennessy's *Eeney, Meeney, Miney, Mo* about four little creatures collecting animals as they romp through the jungle.
   - On another day, read David McPhail's *Snow Lion*, which tells about a hot lion who shares the mountain snows with his jungle animal friends.
2. Jungle animal sounds: Read Rebecca Emberley's *Jungle Sounds*, making the appropriate animal sounds for children to imitate.
3. Jungle walk: Take children on a *Junglewalk* through Nancy Tafuri's wordless book. Walk around the room, stopping now and then as if, like the boy in the book, to look at the magnificent jungle animals and birds.

ART CONNECTIONS

1. A jungle mural: Divide the children into four groups. Cover the walls with colored butcher paper and ask each group to create a jungle mural.
2. Jungle masks: Let children decide what jungle animal they would like to make into a mask. Give them large paper plates (the flimsy kind so that any cutting out will be easy) and help them color, paste on ears, cut out eyes, and affix noses. Patterns for the frog, jackal, rhinoceros, elephant, and leopard can be found in Jan Irving's *Fanfares*.

MUSIC CONNECTIONS

Plan "Deep in the Jungle" from the tape *Deep in the Jungle* by Joe Scruggs. After learning the song, children can act it out.

PUBLISHING

- Display all the books and work that children have made and written.
- Celebrate with a Jungle Party. The party can be as elaborate as the one in Carter's *Surprise Party*, during which children have ice cream, cupcakes, frosty pink punch, and candy, or it can be funny. For instance, have children don their silly party hats and make silly alligators out of gherkins with a raisin for each eye. Reread the book, sing the song "Deep in the Jungle," or show Disney's *Jungle Book*.

Jackdaw 18

SPACE FOOD

Title: *A Trip to Mars.* Orchard Books, 1990.
Author: Ruth Young
Grade level: 3-8
Jackdaw: Chocolate-chip space cookies, carrots, or celery sticks.
Summary: A girl prepares for an imaginary trip to Mars, taking the necessary equipment. The book concludes with a report she wrote.

READING/WRITING CONNECTIONS

1. Begin by opening a space map of the solar system. Place a chalk *X* to mark your location and ask students to imagine going from that *X* to Mars. Explain that that is exactly what Ruth Young did when she wrote *A Trip to Mars.*
2. Read the book. Help children understand how the fictional character's knowledge of Mars helped her choose the objects she planned to take.
3. Talk about the facts presented in the book.
4. Give each student a space cookie (or carrot or celery stick).
5. Explain that students are to begin a "Space Facts Notebook" in which they write about the different things they learn. They may also add drawings to help them remember the facts, just as the girl did in the book.
6. Start the notebooks with a first entry: "Facts I remember after listening to the book *A Trip to Mars.*" Share informally.

—EXTENSIONS—

VOCABULARY/SPELLING

Martian	million	telescope	Phobos	Deimos
gravity	atmosphere	oxygen	wispy	reddish-orange

LIBRARY CONNECTIONS

1. Parts of a book:
   - Point out the double dedication and discuss why there would be two. Talk about the initials *R. Y.* and elicit children's initials, calling attention to capital letters and periods. Talk about the meanings of the two phrases used.
   - Look at the note on the door on the title page and the note on the bed on the last page. Explain that when a beginning and end match or almost match, it is called a "frame." Encourage them to try to create frames for their stories when they write.
2. Areas of the library and fiction/nonfiction: Show children where they can find information on space. Share some nonfiction books on space, such as *Discovering the Stars* by Laurence Santrey or *How Did We Find Out about Comets?* by Isaac Asimov. Juxtapose these with fiction books such as *My Place in Space* by Robin Hirst and Sally Hirst. Help students see that in good fiction books about science there is much fact.

SCIENCE CONNECTIONS

1. Check chapter 22, "Astronomy and Outer Space," in *Science through Children's Literature* by Carol M. Butzow and John W. Butzow for excellent activities and information related to these topics.

2. Learn the astronomical signs and symbols. Write a letter from space telling of your adventures. Instead of giving your place in space in words, use the signs and symbols. Write them in "invisible ink" by using lemon juice as your ink and a toothpick as your pen. When the receiver of your letter irons or heats the paper, your exact position will appear.

MATHEMATICS CONNECTIONS

Inductive and deductive reasoning: Using the book *My Place in Space*, students begin listing from the specific to the general: street address, city or town, state, country, planet, solar system (planets and sun)/solar neighborhood, constellation, galaxy, galaxy group, and universe. Teach them the term *inductive* as a sequencing and thinking tool; then reverse the order to teach *deductive* sequencing and thinking.

LANGUAGE ARTS/ART CONNECTIONS

1. Making books or keeping a journal: Using the information recorded in their Space Facts Notebooks, students write original books on *A Trip to ...*, modeling it on *A Trip to Mars*. What preparations and items would they take to Jupiter with its thick clouds and liquid surface? Invite variations, such as a trip on an asteroid or a comet.

2. Writing letters: For information on the National Aeronautics and Space Administration (NASA), students use their letter-writing skills to write to:
    Superintendent of Documents
    U.S. Government Printing Office
    Washington, DC 20402

3. Drawing space: Students, working in groups, depict the solar system on butcher paper murals after they have studied the relative distances of the planets from the sun.

4. A different point of view: Read *Earthlets as Explained by Professor Xargle* by Jeanne Willis in which babies are described as if they were being studied by someone from outer space. Let students try describing something else common on Earth from Professor Xargle's point of view (for example, a football game).

5. Poetry: Read "The Planet of Mars" in *Where the Sidewalk Ends* by Shel Silverstein. Have students try writing funny poems about something in space and make drawings to accompany the poems.

MUSIC CONNECTIONS

Play the "Mars" segment from Gustav Holst's *The Planets*, op. 32. Students write or draw what they feel while they listen to the music.

PUBLISHING

Create Space Station Day. Display fiction and nonfiction books about all aspects of space as well as students' work. Conclude the celebration with "Taste of Space" tidbits that the students rename in space language. Or eat an "Astronaut's Breakfast" of granola bars, dried fruit, Carnation Instant Breakfast™, Tang™, beef jerky, and apple juice squeezed from Ziploc™ bags.

Jackdaw 19 — CRICKET BOXES

Title: *The Very Quiet Cricket.* Philomel Books, 1990.

Author: Eric Carle

Grade level: Pre-K—5

Jackdaw: An origami cricket box or a small box.

Summary: A little cricket wants to rub his wings together as he meets other insects, but nothing happens. Finally he gets his wish.

READING/WRITING CONNECTIONS

1. Introduce the book with a hand puppet of a cricket or grasshopper. Make the cricket chirp. Ask students to identify this insect and discuss what they already know about crickets.
2. Show them the book's cover and title, inviting speculation as to why the cricket is quiet.
3. Read the book. Let students join in on the predictable line: "But nothing happened. Not a sound." Whisper the part about meeting the other quiet cricket. Then turn the page and let the sound of the cricket delight the children.
4. Read the information about crickets that Carle offers at the book's beginning.
5. Distribute small boxes or give children instructions on how to fold origami cricket boxes. (See a book on origami for directions.)
6. Using Harry Behn's *Cricket Songs* and *More Cricket Songs*, introduce children to haiku about crickets.
7. According to the grade level, students write cricket haiku on small pieces of paper which they fold and put in their cricket boxes. They pair up and either exchange boxes and read each other's haiku, or read their own haiku to their partners. For pre-K and kindergarten, children may draw or write their crickets on small pieces of paper which they fold and put into their boxes.

—EXTENSIONS—

VOCABULARY/SPELLING

cricket	whizzed	locust	praying mantis	scraping
crunched	spittlebug	slurping	froth	cicada
bumblebee	hummed	dragonfly	gliding	mosquitoes
luna moth	sailed	stillness	buzzed	chirped

LIBRARY CONNECTIONS

1. See Jackdaw 1 for information on Eric Carle, his books, and other books on insects.
2. Choral reading: Work up "House Crickets" from *Joyful Noise: Poems for Two Voices* by Paul Fleischman as a choral reading. Use *Fun with Choral Speaking* by Rose Marie Anthony for tips on how to orchestrate the presentation.

3. Read *The Icky Bug Alphabet Book* by Jerry Pallotta. When you get to the "C is for Cricket" page, brainstorm other creatures that begin with the letter *C*.
4. Share pictures of Jiminy Cricket from *The Art of Walt Disney* by Christopher Finch. Compare Disney's cricket with a cricket in a science book. Talk about the likenesses and differences students find.

SCIENCE CONNECTIONS

1. Using the Reading Rainbow Book *Bugs* by Nancy Winslow Parker and Joan Richard Wright or some other book with a good diagram of a cricket, draw a cricket freehand on the blackboard. Children draw crickets at their places. Depending on the grade level, label its parts.
2. Discuss which of the three kinds of crickets—field cricket, house cricket, or tree cricket—is in Eric Carle's book.

LANGUAGE ARTS/ART CONNECTIONS

1. Onomatopoeia: Let the children hear the sound from Carle's book again. Then play "Listen to the Country" by Virginia Pellegrino to hear the cricket sound. In groups of three or four, let children collectively provide the cricket sounds, when you point to them, as you read through *Night in the Country* by Cynthia Rylant.
2. Similes: Read *Quick as a Cricket* by Audrey Wood and Don Wood. Older students may choose other animals and insects about which to create appropriate similes.
3. Circle stories:
   - Cut two large pieces of poster board into circles.
   - On one circle, draw or paste pictures of each of the other insects the cricket met as he journeyed through the story.
   - On the other circle, cut out a pie-shaped wedge big enough to reveal just one of the insects at a time. Draw or paste a picture of the cricket opposite the wedge.
   - Affix the two circles with a large brad fastener.
   - As you reread the story, let children take turns moving the wheel. Invite prediction before actually saying the insect's name.
4. Synonyms for salutations: Examine the multiple ways the little cricket is greeted and brainstorm additional greetings.

Welcome!	Good morning!	Good evening!	Good day!
Good afternoon!	How are you!	Hello!	Good night!
Hi!			

PHYSICAL EDUCATION CONNECTIONS

Children play "Leap Cricket," a variation on the game "Leap Frog" as inspired by the cover of *Quick as a Cricket*.

PUBLISHING

Have a Chirping and Crunching Crickets Celebration by creating a display with all the cricket books, haiku, boxes, pictures, and diagrams. Give all children "cricket crackers" to crunch.

Jackdaw 20   CARDBOARD EGGS

Title: *Too Many Eggs: A Counting Book.* David R. Godine, 1988.

Author: M. Christina Butler

Grade level: Pre-K—K

Jackdaw: Small cardboard eggs traced from the egg pattern in the book.

Summary: Mrs. Bear makes a birthday cake using eggs, but, because she cannot count, the result is funny.

READING/WRITING CONNECTIONS

1. Invite children to speculate about what could happen in a book with the title *Too Many Eggs*. Show the cover and talk about it.
2. As suggested in the book, remove one of the sheets of perforated eggs provided at the beginning of the book. As children count with you, count out the eggs and put them in the basket inside the cupboard provided in the back of the book.
3. Read the book, stopping to count with children the number of eggs Mrs. Bear takes each time from the cupboard to put into her bowls.
4. After the cake is made, Mrs. Bear thinks she only used six eggs. Help children figure out how many eggs she really used by collecting all the eggs from the bowls and counting them as you put them back into the cupboard.
5. Give each child an egg. Divide children into groups and give each group a bowl. Each child puts his or her egg in the bowl and the group then counts the eggs in its bowl. Repeat this process but vary the number of eggs you give the children each time.
6. Have children draw a bowl of eggs and write the number of eggs they have drawn in the bowl.

—EXTENSIONS—

VOCABULARY/SPELLING

eggs	birthday cake	cupboard	basket	bowl
rabbit	badger	owl	squirrel	fox

LIBRARY CONNECTIONS

1. Share other books about eggs:
   - *It Wasn't My Fault* by Helen Lester. Murdley Gurdson tries to find someone to blame when a bird lays an egg on his head.
   - *Egg Thoughts and Other Frances Songs* by Russell Hoban. Verses are about soft-boiled, sunny-side-up, and other methods of preparing eggs.
2. For other activities using eggs, see chapter 1, "Breakfast Starts the Day," in *Mudluscious: Stories and Activities Featuring Food for Preschool Children* by Jan Irving and Robin Currie.

JACKDAW 20—Copyright 1991 Teacher Ideas Press, a division of Libraries Unlimited, Inc., P.O. Box 3988, Englewood, CO 80155-3988

3. Encourage children to say the nursery rhyme "Humpty Dumpty" with you and reenact it by playing the roles of Humpty Dumpty and the king's men.
4. Introduce other counting books:
   - *Counting Sheep* by John Archambault is a colorful rhyming book that reinforces counting from one to ten. Children may mimic each of the animals.
   - *Crows: An Old Rhyme*, with pictures by Heidi Holder, is a number book enriched by research. (See "A Few Words about Weasels, Minks and Crows" at the back of the book.)
   - *Whale Song* by Tony Johnston permits children to repeat and reinforce numbers like an underwater echo.
5. Counting games and rhymes:
   - Use "The Counting Game" in *Play Rhymes*, collected by Marc Brown, which includes illustrations to demonstrate the accompanying physical activities children do as they recite the rhyme.
   - Use "Fish Story," "The Baby Mice," "Five Little Mice," "Two Blackbirds," and "Ten Little Candles" from *Finger Rhymes*, collected by Marc Brown.

SCIENCE CONNECTIONS

1. Examine the consistency of raw, soft-boiled, and hard-boiled eggs.
2. Learn the parts of the egg: Provide each child with an oaktag file folder. They write a title and their name on the cover. The left inside page is for the outside of the egg, the right inside page is for the inside of the egg. The back cover is for "about the author." On the left they draw an oval, labeled "shell," into which they glue pieces of egg shell. The right side is for the yolk and white. Hard-boil enough eggs to give each child an egg slice. Let them first examine their slices like scientists. Then, on the righthand folder page, have them draw their slices which they then color or paint yellow and white. Draw a line from the yolk and label; draw a line from the white and label. Then children may eat their slices!

LANGUAGE ARTS/ART CONNECTIONS

Collect enough egg-shaped containers (from pantyhose packaging) to provide one for each child. Children add their names and decorations to their eggs with colored markers. Then they write "egg" stories and put them inside their eggs.

MATHEMATICS CONNECTIONS

Use the predictable counting book *The Right Number of Elephants* by Jeff Sheppard to have children count backwards from ten to one.

PUBLISHING

Create a display of books around a large Humpty Dumpty with numbers falling around him. Place children's work in the display. On Counting Eggs Day, children read the stories which they take out of their decorated eggs.

Jackdaw 21

YELLOW PAGES

Title: *Frank and Ernest.* Scholastic, 1988.

Author: Alexandra Day

Grade level: All levels

Jackdaw: A page from the Yellow Pages.

Summary: Frank and Ernest begin work in a diner and learn food language.

READING/WRITING CONNECTIONS

1. Give students a food definition list taken from the inside covers of the book. You might include: *Adam's ale*—water, *B and B*—bread and butter, *Burn a snowball*—dip of chocolate ice cream, *Canned cow*—evaporated milk, and *Hen fruit*—egg.

   Talk about the definitions informally, for example, discussing why eggs are called "hen fruit." If a student's parent is a waitress or waiter, that student could research other shorthand terms.

2. Read the book, giving students plenty of time to connect the food language with the real thing. Use *PB & J* (peanut butter and jelly) as an example.

3. Divide the students into groups according to their Yellow Page ads. As a group, they compile a list of words related to those ads and derive a new language to define those words. They may borrow some from *Frank and Ernest*, but encourage them to think creatively. For example:

   - Students with Yellow Pages about cars form a group.
   - List things pertaining to cars, such as "steering wheel," "motor," "trunk."
   - Create the "new language" definitions, such as "hand swivel," "the drive ride," and "the elephant's nose." (To extend this even more, definitions could be presented in the context of a sentence or even a story.)
   - Share with the class. If anyone does not understand, the group should be ready to explain.

—EXTENSIONS—

VOCABULARY/SPELLING

idioms	homophones	homonyms	rebuses
riddles	proverbs	puns	limericks

LIBRARY CONNECTIONS

1. Fun with language: Immerse students in language play by using books showing that language can be fun.

   - *Idioms*—Use *Amelia Bedelia* by Peggy Parish to teach idiom. Invite students to do an eight-page book on original idioms. (See Jackdaw 4 for directions on how to fold an eight-page book.)
   - *Homophones*—Use *One Whole Doughnut, One Doughnut Hole* by Valjean McLenighan and invite eight-page books on other homophones.
   - *Limericks*—Use *The Book of Pigericks: Pig Limericks* by Arnold Lobel and encourage eight-page books of original limericks.

JACKDAW 21—Copyright 1991 Teacher Ideas Press, a division of Libraries Unlimited, Inc., P.O. Box 3988, Englewood, CO 80155-3988

- *Puns*—Use the sophisticated alphabet book *The Weighty Word Book* by Paul M. Levitt, Douglas A. Burger, and Elissa S. Guralnick to introduce students to elongated puns. Students could try their hand at writing one of these "weighty word" stories.
- *Proverbs/Clichés*—Use *First Things First: An Illustrated Collection of Sayings* by Betty Fraser to introduce students to some familiar proverbs and their meanings. (On an upper grade level, this same book could be used when working with cliché.)
- *Puns, riddles, and rebuses*—Use *Puniddles* by Bruce McMillan and Brett McMillan for fun with riddles solved through visual puns. Students, working in pairs, may try to find pictures that, put together, form other "puniddles." These word puzzles could also be used as an example of a sophisticated rebus.
- *Rebuses*—Use *Who Stole the Apples* by Sigrid Heuck to captivate younger children through delightfully bright word pictures. Children could make an eight-page book with rebus sentences.
- *Homonyms*—Use *A Chocolate Moose for Dinner* by Fred Gwynne for work with homonyms. Students can make an eight-page book of homonyms following Gwynne's style.

2. Show students the area of the library where they can find other books dealing with language. Older students may enjoy exploring these suggestions:
   - *Word Origins: The Romance of Language* by Cecil Hunt gives background on the Achilles of "Achilles' heel," the Adam of "Adam's apple," and the Croesus in "as rich as Croesus." Students could make an eight-page book of modern etymologies.
   - *American Talk: The Words and Ways of American Dialects* by Robert Hendrickson provides a potpourri of information, from English words that came from other languages, such as the Australian "boomerang," the French "pumpkin," and the Hawaiian "tattoo" to "rappin" black-style and discombobulating twists. Students could create a slang dictionary.
   - *More on Oxymoron* by Patrick Hughes contains a plethora of verbal and visual pleonasms, oxymorons, contradictions, nothings, and more. Students could write (and draw or find pictures) for a sequel to Hughes's book.
   - *The Well-Tempered Sentence: A Punctuation Handbook for the Innocent, the Eager, and the Doomed* by Karen Elizabeth Gordon might cause even the most recalcitrant students to learn some things about language. For example, "In Spanish, the exclamation point comes before the sentence, inverted, as well as after it, right end up." Students, following Gordon's model, could make a version for elementary students.

PUBLISHING

Display all the books on language juxtaposing the students' versions with their models. Have a read-around in which students sit in a circle and each reads several pages from his or her book in turn.

Jackdaw 22 — WATERMELONS

Title: *The Enormous Watermelon.* Rigby, 1986 (reprinted 1989).

Author: Retold by Brenda Parks and Judith Smith

Grade level: Pre-K—1

Jackdaw: A piece of watermelon.

Summary: In this big book, Old Mother Hubbard plants a watermelon seed. When the melon is ready to be picked, it is so enormous that she calls, one by one, other nursery-rhyme characters to help her pick it.

READING/WRITING CONNECTIONS

1. Show children the book and discuss how the story, about a "big," enormous watermelon, is like the oversized book. Talk about watermelons.
2. Ask children to tell you what the woman on the book's cover is doing. Tell them that the woman is Old Mother Hubbard; recite the nursery rhyme to remind them about Old Mother Hubbard and invite them to join in.
3. Read the book. Take advantage of the three-quarter-page format, which hints about the next nursery-rhyme character to appear by encouraging students to examine the clues and predict the characters. Reread the book so that children join in on the repetitions and make the predictions with more confidence.
4. Give children pieces of watermelon. After they have eaten, distribute large pieces of construction paper to be folded into thirds. In the top panel, children draw a small green melon shape; in the middle panel they draw a big green melon shape; in the bottom panel they draw a bigger green melon shape. They then write and share stories about a growing watermelon.

—EXTENSIONS—

VOCABULARY/SPELLING

Old Mother Hubbard	Humpty Dumpty	watermelon
Little Miss Muffet	juicy	grew
Jack and Jill	enormous	pulled
Willy Winky	picked	kitchen

LIBRARY CONNECTIONS

1. Share other big books:
   - Use *Time for a Rhyme*, illustrated by Marjory Gardner, Heather Philpott, and Jane Tanner, to reinforce the nursery rhymes and to permit children to identify some of the characters mentioned in *The Enormous Watermelon*.
   - Use *Hattie and the Fox* by Mem Fox to reinforce shared reading and predicting.

2. Introduce other sequencing books, such as *The Day Jimmy's Boa Ate the Wash* and *Jimmy's Boa and the Big Splash Birthday Bash* by Trinka Hakes Noble.

3. Show children where oversize books are kept in the library. Encourage them to play librarian and read them to their friends.

4. Choral refrain: Encourage children to repeat the "grew" and "pulled" refrains by controlling their voices. Teach them to whisper, use their normal voices, then make their voices louder. Call attention to the way the print gets bigger when voices should get louder. Talk about the sounds for *gr* and *p*.

5. Check *Fun with Choral Speaking* by Rose Marie Anthony for an entire section on "Mother Goose Rhymes" and *One Potato, Two Potato, Three Potato, Four: 165 Chants for Children*, compiled by Mary Lou Colgin, for a wide selection of nursery rhymes. Use *Each Peach Pear Plum* by Janet Ahlberg and Allan Ahlberg to find more nursery-rhyme characters.

LANGUAGE ARTS CONNECTIONS

1. Dialog: Show children the red print and explain that the red print means that Old Mother Hubbard is talking. Read those sections in an Old Mother Hubbard voice.

2. Story mural: Tape a long sheet of butcher paper to the wall. Make a section for the title and author, a section for the characters, and a series of horizontal blocks. Then invite children to retell the story as you write what they say in the blocks. When Old Mother Hubbard talks, put the words in "little lips" and write her words in red (or you can let a child go over the quotation marks in red, with lipstick, for instance).

SCIENCE CONNECTIONS

1. Things that grow on vines: Brainstorm a list of things that grow on vines. Plant the seeds of a melon and chart what happens. See *Pumpkin Pumpkin* by Jeanne Titherington for a description of a growing gourd.

2. Gourds: Watermelons are part of the gourd family. Bring in other species for exhibit.

3. Parts of a watermelon: Classify the parts of a watermelon—skin, rind, fleshy center, and seeds.

4. Learn the colors of watermelon: Make a Watermelon Color Chart of red, pink, yellow, and white.

5. Reinforce letters: Use *Eating the Alphabet* by Lois Ehlert (see Jackdaw 7).

ART CONNECTIONS

Make papier-mâché watermelons of different sizes. Paint some in stripes and some in solid colors of green.

MUSIC CONNECTIONS

Use *Go In and Out the Window* (music arranged and edited by Dan Fox) for the music, words, and art for many classic nursery rhymes.

PUBLISHING

Make a Watermelon Patch. With *The Enormous Watermelon* in the center, display all the other books used and work children have done. Place the papier-mâché watermelons around the books and writing. Cut out paper vines, leaves, and tendrils to arrange in and around the display.

JACKDAW 22—Copyright 1991 Teacher Ideas Press, a division of Libraries Unlimited, Inc., P.O. Box 3988, Englewood, CO 80155-3988

Jackdaw 23

NEWSPAPERS

Title: *The Furry News: How to Make a Newspaper.* Holiday House, 1990.

Author: Loreen Leedy

Grade level: 3-6

Jackdaw: A newspaper (try to obtain different kinds, issues, and sizes).

Summary: Several animals work hard to write, edit, and print their own newspaper.

READING/WRITING CONNECTIONS

1. Distribute the newspapers. Ask the students what section they would read first and discuss why.
2. Call attention to the newspaper's physical characteristics: size, number of columns per page, pictures, lead story, number of pages, and use of color, if any.
3. Before reading the book, invite students to decide what part of the newspaper they would like to work on while you read.
4. After the reading, get a sampling of what students would like to work on, but tell them that first they will all be reporters.
5. Divide students into pairs. Give each reporter five minutes to interview his or her partner about a favorite activity or hobby. Then allow ten minutes for reporters to write up a brief feature article to present to the class.

—EXTENSIONS—

VOCABULARY/SPELLING

Students become familiar with all the newspaper terms in the glossary.

LIBRARY CONNECTIONS

1. Visit the newspaper section of a large library and count how many different newspapers they handle each day.
2. Research newspapers in the United States. Write for samples.
3. Research the "Code of Ethics" for journalists.
4. Show the parts of the book, especially noting the glossary. Discuss the function of the glossary.

SCIENCE CONNECTIONS

1. Weather: Students, working in groups, become "experts" on aspects of the weather:
   - *Group one*—Graphs the city or town's high and low temperatures for a week or a month.
   - *Group two*—Graphs the state's high and low temperatures for a week or a month.
   - *Group three*—Graphs the high and low temperatures for the United States for a week or a month.
   - *Group four*—Clips out the newspaper's forecast, then assesses its accuracy each day.

2. Habitats: Students work in three groups—the Ocean group, the Fresh Water group, or the Land group—to find articles related to life in their assigned areas.

3. Plants and animals: Students work in either the Plant group or the Animal group to find newspaper articles related to plants and their uses or animals and their uses.

MATHEMATICS CONNECTIONS

1. Working with measurements: Find an article or an ad with measurements. For example, an article on the sports page may talk about yards gained or lost in a game. Convert those measurements to other units, such as inches or feet.

2. Basing problems on real ads: Using an ad for carpet or tile, measure the floor of the classroom in order to figure out how much carpet or tile to buy and how much it would cost.

LANGUAGE ARTS CONNECTIONS

1. Word choice/diction: Students work in one of three groups—the Noun group, the Verb group, or the Adjective group—to find a good example of "their" words. They share their example and why they think it is a good example of word choice. (You can rotate students so that all students eventually get into each different group.)

2. Write an article using the Reporter's Formula: Who? What? When? Where? Why? How?

3. Interview someone for a feature article that will be published in the newspaper.

4. Find ads that spell brand names in unconventional ways, such as *SAVX*. Discuss acronyms.

5. Use advice columns and letters to the editor to reteach letter-writing.

6. Have students act as proofreaders and search for mistakes in the newspaper.

SOCIAL STUDIES CONNECTIONS

1. Clip maps out of newspapers and compare to those in encyclopedias and textbooks.

2. Discuss propaganda devices such as bandwagon, slogans, repetition, loaded words, powerful images, and emotional appeals. Discuss how these can affect prejudices.

ART CONNECTIONS

Make a collage of newspaper headlines, editorial cartoons, or pictures.

PUBLISHING

Let students write, edit, and publish their own class newspaper, using the model of the animals in *The Furry News*. Follow the directions given on the two-page spread entitled "Making Your Own Newspaper for Your Family, Neighborhood or School." Display these newspapers on a bulletin board captioned "WE KNOW HOW TO MAKE A NEWSPAPER"; cut the caption's letters out of a newspaper.

Jackdaw 24

RED KITES

Title: *Who Said Red?* Margaret K. McElderry Books, 1988.

Author: Mary Serfozo

Grade level: Pre-K—1

Jackdaw: A small red paper kite or red kite stickers.

Summary: One child keeps insisting on the color *red* while another child asks about other colors.

READING/WRITING CONNECTIONS

1. Wear something red the day you introduce this book. Talk about red that you and the children are wearing, shades of red, and red in the room.
2. Have self-sticking notes ready with the word RED written on them. Let children stick them onto different red items in the room.
3. Show the book's red cover. Invite the children to look closely at the picture. Talk about what is happening and speculate on what might happen next.
4. Read the book. Then reread, this time inviting children to join in with the appropriate color names.
5. Distribute the small paper kites. Ask children to write about their favorite red food, toy, book, or article of clothing. When they are finished, staple the paper kites on the top of their papers.

—EXTENSIONS—

VOCABULARY/SPELLING

red	green	blue	yellow	purple
brown	pink	orange	black	white

LIBRARY CONNECTIONS

1. Share other books about color:
   - Read *Mouse Paint* by Ellen Stoll Walsh and *Little Blue and Little Yellow* by Leo Lionni to explore with children the delight in creating colors.
   - Read the poems in *Hailstones and Halibut Bones: Adventures in Colors* by Mary O'Neill to alert children to all the different things that can be one color. Alternatives are Shel Silverstein's "Colors" in *Where the Sidewalk Ends* and "Why the Sky Is Blue" by John Ciardi in *Fast and Slow*.
   - Read *Color Farm* and *Color Zoo* by Lois Ehlert to show children how to use color and form to make animals.
   - Read *Clifford: The Big Red Dog* by Norman Bridwell to reinforce the color red.
   - Read *Mary Wore Her Red Dress and Henry Wore His Green Sneakers*, adapted by Merle Peek, to reinforce learning many of the colors used in *Who Said Red?*

JACKDAW 24—Copyright 1991 Teacher Ideas Press, a division of Libraries Unlimited, Inc., P.O. Box 3988, Englewood, CO 80155-3988

- Read *The Rainbow Goblins* by Ul de Rico to tell the story of the colors of the rainbow and why it never touches earth.
- Read *Elmer* by David McKee to summarize the work on color with a delightful story about a colorful elephant.

2. Introduce the encyclopedia: Take children to the reference section of the library. Look up rainbows in the encyclopedia and read to them about why we have colors and how rainbows happen.

SCIENCE CONNECTIONS

1. Flying kites: Divide children into groups and let each group fly a kite. See which one can fly the highest. Talk about what makes kites fly and what probably happened to the boy's kite in the story.

2. Turning a stalk of celery red: Perform the experiment by filling a cup with water, adding red food coloring, and standing a freshly cut stalk of celery in the water. Discuss why the stalk is red the next day.

LANGUAGE ARTS/ART CONNECTIONS

1. Synecdoche: Introduce children to synecdoche—a part for the whole—by using *Purple Is Part of a Rainbow* by Carolyn Kowalczyk. Let children orally create other parts of whole things as a game.

2. Form and meaning: Use the Ehlert books to encourage students to make animal-face kites out of colored tissue paper. Ask students where their kites will fly.

3. Allusion: Show children the book *The Red Thread* by Tord Nygren. Let them "follow the red thread" through this wordless book and discuss what they see. They may recognize some of their favorite characters from literature. Give them red yarn to paste on a page on which they have drawn meaningful pictures, like ones in the book.

4. Direct address: Read *The Little Mouse, the Red Ripe Strawberry, and the Big Hungry Bear* by Don Wood and Audrey Wood. Invite children to mime the actions of the little mouse. Conclude by sharing strawberry halves with children.

MUSIC CONNECTIONS

Sing the Texas folk song "Mary Wore Her Red Dress" using variations on the clothing and the colors. As children grow familiar with the song, they can change to weather, animals, or other topics.

SOCIAL STUDIES CONNECTIONS

Show children a large wall map of the United States. Tracing your route with a ruler or pointer, tell children the adventures of your kite. Invite children to do the same.

PUBLISHING

Celebrate Red Day during Rainbow Week! Each day, invite children to wear or bring something in the day's designated color. (Make certain you have name tags or something of the proper color for those who forget.) Celebrate each color through stories, poems, and songs such as "Lavender's Blue" and "Red River Valley" from *Go In and Out the Window* by Dan Fox.

Jackdaw 25

LETTERS

Title: *The Jolly Postman or Other People's Letters.* Little, Brown, 1986.

Author: Allan Ahlberg and Janet Ahlberg

Grade level: All levels

Jackdaw: A piece of stationery and an envelope.

Summary: A jolly postman delivers appropriate mail to fairy-tale characters.

READING/WRITING CONNECTIONS

1. Begin by brainstorming a list of fairy-tale characters.
2. Ask children, if they were to write to one of these characters, which one it would be, why they would choose that one, and what they would say.
3. Show them the book and see if they can identify all the characters on the cover. (Even older students will love this book for its punning.)
4. Read through the book. Let younger students actually take the mail out of the envelopes. Talk about each of the characters and review their stories.
5. Distribute the stationery and envelopes and allow students to write a letter to the storybook character of their choice. Share as each student takes a turn sitting in the Author's Chair.

—EXTENSIONS—

VOCABULARY/SPELLING

porridge   magician   occupant   bungalow   hobgoblin   covens

LIBRARY CONNECTIONS

1. Introduce other books:
   - *A Book of Boxes* by Laura Mason has pages of boxes that open, revealing removable items to delight children.
   - *My Presents*, written and illustrated by Rod Campbell, has wrapped presents with word hints about the contents that can be opened, although the items cannot be removed.
   - *Letters of Thanks: A Christmas Tale* by Manghanita Kempadoo is a series of letters by a Katherine Huntington to a Lord Gilbert, thanking him for each of the gifts of the twelve days of Christmas.
2. Corpus of work by an author: Check *Bookpeople: A First Album* by Sharron L. McElmeel for biographical information on the Ahlbergs. Gather books by the Ahlbergs and discuss ways in which each book is special.

   The Clothes Horse and Other Stories   *Funnybones*
   Each Peach Pear Plum (see Jackdaw 22)   *Jeremiah in the Dark Woods*
3. Share a sampling of other books of and about letters:

   The Best of Dear Abby by Abigail Van Buren
   Ernest Hemingway: Selected Letters 1917-1961 (Carlos Baker, ed.)
   Love Letters: An Illustrated Anthology (Antonia Fraser, ed.)

LANGUAGE ARTS CONNECTIONS

1. Letter writing: Write to the Ahlbergs—

   c/o Viking Kestrel
   536 King Road
   London, SW 10 OUH
   England

   c/o Viking Penguin, Inc.
   40 West 23rd Street
   New York, NY 10010

2. Persuasive letters: Write to a customer relations manager or consumer affairs office about a legitimate concern or complaint, using the proper form.

3. Friendly letters: Write a friendly letter to a friend or relative.

4. Letter-writing to literary characters: Make a book of letters, following the model of *The Jolly Postman*, to literary characters students are studying. For example, they may write to Macbeth, Lady Macbeth, Duncan, Scout, or Harper Lee. This is best done as a series of letters.

5. Pen pals: Check *All about Letters* for lists of sources for pen pals.

SOCIAL STUDIES CONNECTIONS

1. History of the United States Postal Service: Send for *All about Letters* (revised edition) from NCTE. This 64-page book, produced by the U.S. Postal Service in cooperation with the National Council of Teachers of English, contains much interesting and invaluable information on the history of the Postal Service.

2. History in letters:
   - *The Book of Abigail and John: Selected Letters of the Adams Family, 1762-1784* (L. H. Butterfield, Marc Friedlander, and Mary-Jo Kline, eds.).
   - *The Children of Pride* (Robert Manson Myers, ed.).
   - *A Letter to Anywhere* by Al Hine and John Alcorn. This book contains the history of letter-writing around the world and over the centuries.
   - *Letters in American History: Words to Remember* (H. Jack Lang, ed.).

MUSIC CONNECTIONS

Share books that deal with letters from musicians:
- *Letters of Beethoven* (3 vols., translated by Emily Anderson).
- *Letters to a Musical Boy* by Mervyn Bruxner.
- *Letters to Horseface: Being the Story of Wolfgang Amadeus Mozart's Journey to Italy, 1769-1770, When He Was a Boy of Fourteen* by F. M. Monjo.

PUBLISHING

Celebrate a Red-Letter Day by displaying all the books about letters and all the students' letters. Give the students letter stickers and letter stamps. (This is more fun to do around Valentine's Day.)

Jackdaw 26 — CEREAL ALPHABET LETTERS

Title: *The Book of Shadowboxes: The Story of the ABC's.* Peachtree Publishers, 1990.

Author: Laura L. Seeley

Grade level: All levels

Jackdaw: A cereal alphabet letter.

Summary: Each letter is introduced through rhythm, rhyme, alliteration, repetition, and items beginning with that letter arranged in a shadowbox.

READING/WRITING CONNECTIONS

1. Begin by showing students a shadowbox. Talk about the objects in the box and discuss the purpose of shadowboxes.
2. Show the cover of the book.
3. Read the delightful dedication and discuss the way Seeley uses language in it: "Buddy, who'll window the panes and candy the canes...."
4. Read the poem that introduces "Shadow." Point out that there will be extra things to see. Name the object and see who can spot it first.
5. Read the book, allowing time for the students to savor its richness.
6. Students then pick a cereal alphabet letter from a bag or bowl and list items that begin with that letter. Then, following Seeley's model, they draw a shadowbox and either write or draw in the items that begin with their letter.
7. After they make their shadowboxes, they compose rhymes to match.

—EXTENSIONS—

VOCABULARY/SPELLING

avocado	artichoke	armadillo	alligator	buzzing	bugle
cricket	camel	candle	dinosaur	dalmation	dolphin
envelopes	eclair	flamingo	french fries	giraffe	gerbil
guitar	genuine	guppies	hyena	horizon	igloo
iguana	jaguar	kookaburra	ketchup	khaki	lizard
leprechaun	leopard	mouse	moose	moustache	musical
nostrils	nickel	octagons	ostrich	pepperoni	pelican
quarrels	quivering	rascally	rustic	raisins	sneaky
shovel	teepee	toucan	urn	ukulele	unkempt
urchin	umbrella	versatile	vulnerable	voracious	vitamins
walrus	whispering	whiskers	saxophone	pixies	tuxedo
yuccas	yacht	yogurt	yodeling	zeppelin	zebu

JACKDAW 26—Copyright 1991 Teacher Ideas Press, a division of Libraries Unlimited, Inc., P.O. Box 3988, Englewood, CO 80155-3988

LIBRARY CONNECTIONS

1. Share other alphabet books (see Jackdaws 6, 7, and 9).
2. Share antique alphabet books:
   - *A: Apple Pie: An Old Fashioned Alphabet Book* by Kate Greenaway delights all ages.
   - "An Alphabetical Arrangement of Animals for Little Naturalists" and "The Alphabet of Goody Two Shoes" in *A Treasury of Illustrated Children's Books: Early Nineteenth-Century Classics from the Osborne Collection* by Leonard De Vries helps students see the alphabet from a historical perspective. (See also Jackdaws 6, 7, and 9.)

SCIENCE CONNECTIONS

1. Share *Animalia* by Graeme Base for reinforcement of the alphabet as well as the beauty of the animal illustrations. Have students make an ABC book of animals they are studying.

LANGUAGE ARTS/ART CONNECTIONS

1. Egg-carton shadowboxes: Each student makes a shadowbox by putting objects that begin with his or her designated letter in the egg compartments. They may write a rhyme and affix it to the lid.
2. Spatter-paint letters: Cut out a letter from cardboard and tape it on a paper plate. Put newspaper around the work area. Dip a toothbrush in tempera paint and run it back and forth over a small piece of screen held above the plate. When the paint dries and the letter is removed from the plate, it will appear in silhouette.
3. Alliteration, adjectives, and adverbs:
   - Use *The Book of Shadowboxes* as an introduction to the poetic device of alliteration. ("A Kettle's for the Kitchen" in *Sing a Song of Popcorn*, selected by Beatrice Schenk de Regniers, is also good for alliteration.)

SOCIAL STUDIES CONNECTIONS

Use *ABC: The Wild West Buffalo Bill Historical Center, Cody, Wyoming* by Florence Cassen Mayers, which illustrates each letter of the alphabet with one or more objects from the Buffalo Bill Historical Center. Students may make an ABC book of artifacts, objects, and people from any period in history with a brief explanation included on each page. They may do the same for their own classrooms. These can be "leather-bound" to give an authentic look:

- Paste small pieces of masking tape every which way over one side (the outer side) of two pieces of very stiff cardboard.
- Use some fabric scraps as wipes to spread tan, brown, or black paste shoe polish over the tape. Wipe away excess and let stand overnight.
- Cover the other side (the inside) of the cardboard with decorative paper.
- Put the alphabet pages inside and affix with tape, staples, or chicken rings (plastic rings, available from feed stores, which are used to tag chickens).

PHYSICAL EDUCATION CONNECTIONS

Use *A My Name Is ALICE* by Jane Bayer to reinforce the alphabet and to work with motor skills (directions given by author at the book's conclusion).

PUBLISHING

Display all the alphabet books and the students' work around and in an enlarged shadowbox, which can be constructed with cardboard on the bulletin board or on a table.

JACKDAW 26—Copyright 1991 Teacher Ideas Press, a division of Libraries Unlimited, Inc., P.O. Box 3988, Englewood, CO 80155-3988

Jackdaw 27 — PLAY MONEY

Title: *If You Made a Million.* Lothrop, Lee & Shepard Books, 1989.

Author: David M. Schwartz

Grade level: 3-12

Jackdaw: Play money.

Summary: This book describes money in its various forms and explains how money can be used to buy things, pay off loans, and build interest.

READING/WRITING CONNECTIONS

1. Before showing the book, take one of its lines, "Making money means making choices," and ask students what they would do with the money if they made a million dollars. Talk about their choices.
2. Show the cover. Point out "Marvelosissimo the Mathematical Magician" and invite speculation about why Steven Kellogg, the illustrator, used him and other fantasy creations on the cover of a book about money.
3. Discuss the reality of the copyright page and the fantasy of the title page.
4. As you read, invite suggestions of things that could be purchased for the given money amounts other than those offered in the book.
5. When you have finished, have students dip into the "money bag" for some denomination of play money. Some will receive a higher denomination than others, but each is to follow the book's model by writing three things:
   - How they earned that specific amount.
   - What they would do with it.
   - Why they made that choice.
6. Share students' writing informally in groups. Each group chooses a "best of group," based not on the highest denomination but on the quality and creativity of the choices. "Best of group" is shared with the entire class.

—EXTENSIONS—

VOCABULARY/SPELLING

penny	nickel	dollar	hundred	interest
compound interest	quarter	checks	checking accounts	loans
income tax	thousand	million	obstreperous ogres	denomination

LIBRARY CONNECTIONS

1. Share some of the interesting information found in "A Note from the Author: What Would We Do without Money?" in the back of the book.
2. Share the companion book, *How Much Is a Million?*, which takes the abstract concepts of million, billion, and trillion and makes them fun and understandable.

JACKDAW 27—Copyright 1991 Teacher Ideas Press, a division of Libraries Unlimited, Inc., P.O. Box 3988, Englewood, CO 80155-3988

3. Read *The Hundred Penny Box* by Sharon Bell Mathis.

MATHEMATICS CONNECTIONS

1. Check Ruth Joslyn's article "Using Concrete Models to Teach Large Number Concepts," for connections to *How Much Is a Million?*
2. Writing checks/writing out numbers: Give students specific amounts. Students must use those amounts to reinforce writing certain numbers, but they may make out their checks to whomever they wish.
3. Shopping: Distribute catalogs and have students compile a "wish list" of all the things they would buy from the catalogs. Add up the figures to compute a class total. How many classes could spend that much before it totalled a million?
4. Keeping a register: Students receive a page from a ledger showing a large amount of money. They are then given priced items to subtract from the amount in their ledgers.
5. Students, working in groups, create word problems based on money which other groups work to figure out.
6. Other ideas about banks, interest, compound interest, checks, checking accounts, loans, income tax, and problems using measurement, weight, and calculations dealing with volume can be found in the back of the book.

SOCIAL STUDIES CONNECTIONS

1. Trading: Divide students into groups. Each group decides what common or relatively rare objects they could use as a basis for their money system (for example, pebbles, beans, colored paper). They then barter with other groups.
2. Research the history of money.
3. Invite a numismatist to speak to the class. Help students realize that coins preserve old forms of writing and provide clues about history through the portraits of eminent persons.

SCIENCE CONNECTIONS

After students collect cans for recycling, they weigh the cans and compute the money they will make. Together they determine a positive environmental project upon which to spend the earned money (for example, buying a tree for the school ground).

MUSIC CONNECTIONS

Divide the class into teams. Working under a specified time limit, each team brainstorms and researches all the songs, poems, and nursery rhymes that have money or some denomination of money in the title.

PUBLISHING

Celebrate Millionaire Day by displaying books, students' writing, and computations about money.

JACKDAW 27—Copyright 1991 Teacher Ideas Press, a division of Libraries Unlimited, Inc., P.O. Box 3988, Englewood, CO 80155-3988

Jackdaw 28 — CARDBOARD CIRCLES

Title: *Earth Circles.* Walker, 1989.

Author: Sandra Ure Griffin

Grade level: All levels

Jackdaw: A cardboard circle.

Summary: A mother and daughter celebrate the cycles of nature on the first day of spring.

READING/WRITING CONNECTIONS

1. Hold up a circle and ask students what they think when they see a circle. Probe (according to grade level) for its symbolism, particularly the notion that a circle has no beginning and no end.
2. Explain that making a circle helps people make concrete the abstract cycles of nature. Ask students to think of natural cycles.
3. Read the book. Invite different students to read the words written around the circles. They will catch the rhythm and cyclical pattern.
4. Distribute circles. Students draw or paint the sun on one side, the moon on the other. Then they write something cyclical, something that can be read again and again around one or both sides.
5. Share these circles in a read-a-round: As students and teacher sit in circle formation, begin anywhere and simply read around.

—EXTENSIONS—

VOCABULARY/SPELLING

spring	summer	autumn	winter	slender	caterpillar
cocoon	blanket	shimmering	vanishes	dwindles	married

LIBRARY CONNECTIONS

1. Tell about the author:
   - Explain that this is Sandra Ure Griffin's first book. Show the copyright page and read the explanation of how she achieved the art for this book. Talk about how the art in the book reinforces its meaning and how form and meaning merge.
   - Read and discuss Griffin's words, "I believe there is a bond between parent and child that is as strong and endless as all forces of nature. Generation to generation, the cycles of love never end."
2. Share other books on this theme:
   - *Mama, Were You Ever Young?* by John Hay defines the nature of youth in lively rhyme and meter.
   - *The Fall of Freddie the Leaf* by Leo Buscaglia captures the magic of nature through the passing of seasons.
   - *Grandfather Twilight* by Barbara Berger pictures the natural cycle of daylight to dark.
   - *The Stranger* by Chris Van Allsburg chronicles in allegory the cycle of changing seasons.

- *Now One Foot, Now the Other* by Tomie de Paola touchingly tells the cycle of a boy's relationship with his grandfather.
- *David's Little Indian* by Margaret Wise Brown helps students appreciate each day through the seasons.
- *Old Henry* by Joan W. Blos captures the rhythm of people learning to get along.
- *I'm in Charge of Celebrations* by Byrd Baylor shares the cycle of private celebrations.
- *Many Moons* by James Thurber wisely and humorously stresses the acceptance of cycles in life.

3. Share read-around books:
   - *If You Give a Mouse a Cookie* by Laura Joffe Numeroff relates a cycle of requests and can be read again and again.
   - *The House on Main Street* by Arnold Shapiro is a story told in a read-around pop-up book.

SCIENCE CONNECTIONS

1. Seasons: Keep an ongoing section in the room where the students collect natural things (or pictures and books of natural things) that convey the different seasons. Return to this as the seasons or books warrant.
2. Day/night: Keep monthly or weekly charts on the time of the sunrise and sunset. Use the newspaper or television weather channel for sources.

LANGUAGE ARTS/ART CONNECTIONS

1. Symbolism: Study the symbolic use of circles in literature, using poems such as e.e. cummings's concrete poem, "O Moon How Do You Float?"
2. Poetry and art: Read poems from Jane Yolen's *Ring of Earth: A Child's Book of Seasons* while displaying the rich illustrations, then divide students into triads. Each triad receives a large piece of butcher paper which has been cut into a circle. The group plans:
   - What its cycle will convey (its message). This could be linked to other literature or stories being studies.
   - What its cycle will include: animals, plants, people, abstractions.
   - The cycle's design and medium: tempera, tissue art, collage, or other.

   When the group cycles are finished, display them for the whole class.

SOCIAL STUDIES CONNECTIONS

Compile genealogy charts of students' families to give them a sense of the cycle of their own families. Study genealogy charts of historical or literary figures.

MATHEMATICS CONNECTIONS

To practice measurement and diameter, make a circle book:
- Cut four to ten pieces of paper into eight-inch circles.
- Draw a line on one for its diameter.
- Paper-clip all the circles together.
- Sew a seam with dental floss along the diameter.

PUBLISHING

Write a cycle or a read-around story in students' circle books. Display these and all the other books in circle formations around the room.

JACKDAW 28—Copyright 1991 Teacher Ideas Press, a division of Libraries Unlimited, Inc., P.O. Box 3988, Englewood, CO 80155-3988

BIBLIOGRAPHY

Aardema, Verna. *Bringing the Rain to Kapiti Plain.* New York: Dial Books for Young Readers, 1981.

Ahlberg, Allan, and Janet Ahlberg. *The Clothes Horse and Other Stories.* New York: Penguin Books, 1988; *Each Peach Pear Plum.* New York: Puffin Books, 1978; *Funnybones.* New York: Greenwillow Books, 1981; *Jeremiah in the Dark Woods.* New York: Viking, 1987; *The Jolly Postman or Other People's Letters.* Boston: Little, Brown, 1986; *How a Book Is Made.* New York: Harper & Row, 1986.

All about Letters. United States Postal Service and NCTE (available from National Council of Teachers of English, 1111 Kenyon Road, Urbana, IL 61801), 1982.

Allen, Trena. *Peeking Out of a Tree.* Allen, Tex.: DLM Teaching Resources, 1989.

Anderson, Emily, trans. *Letters of Beethoven.* London: Macmillan, 1961.

Angelou, Maya. *Now Sheba Sings the Song.* New York: E. P. Dutton/Dial, 1987.

Anno, Mitsumasa. *Anno's Peekaboo.* New York: Philomel Books, 1987.

Anthony, Rose Marie. *Fun with Choral Speaking.* Englewood, Colo.: Libraries Unlimited, 1990.

Archambault, John. *Counting Sheep.* New York: Henry Holt, 1989.

Asch, Frank. *Bear Shadow.* New York: Simon & Schuster, 1988; *Happy Birthday, Moon.* New York: Simon & Schuster, 1988; *I Can Blink.* New York: Crown Publishers, 1985; *I Can Roar.* New York: Crown Publishers, 1986; *Moon Bear.* New York: Scribner & Sons, 1978; *Popcorn.* New York: Parent's Magazine Read Aloud Books, 1979; *Sand Cake.* New York: Parent's Magazine Read Aloud Books, 1987; *Skyfire.* New York: Simon & Schuster Books for Young Readers, 1984.

Asimov, Isaac. *How Did We Find Out about Comets?* New York: Walker, 1975.

Bains, Rae. *Simple Machines.* Mahwah, N.J.: Troll Associates, 1985.

Baker, Carlos, ed. *Ernest Hemingway: Selected Letters (1917-1961).* New York: Macmillan, 1989.

Base, Graeme. *Animalia.* New York: Henry N. Abrams, 1987.

Bass, Saul. *Why Man Creates* (film). Kaiser Aluminum & Chemical Corp., 1968.

Bayer, Jane. *A My Name Is ALICE.* New York: Dial Books for Young Readers, 1984.

Baylor, Byrd. *Amigo.* New York: Aladdin Books, 1989; *The Best Town in the World.* New York: Aladdin Books, 1982; *The Desert Is Theirs.* New York: Aladdin Books, 1986; *Everybody Needs a Rock.* New York: Aladdin Books, 1974; *Feet!* Illustrated by Peter Parnall. New York: Macmillan, 1988; *Guess Who My Favorite Person Is.* New York: Aladdin Books, 1977; *Hawk, I'm Your Brother.* New York: Aladdin Books, 1986; *If You Are a Hunter of Fossils.* New York: Aladdin Books, 1980; *I'm in Charge of Celebrations.* New York: Charles Scribner's Sons, 1986; *The Way to Start a Day.* New York: Aladdin Books, 1986; *When the Clay Sings.* New York: Aladdin Books, 1972.

Behn, Harry. *Cricket Songs: Japanese Haiku.* New York: Harcourt, Brace & World, 1964; *More Cricket Songs.* New York: Harcourt Brace Jovanovich, 1971.

Belloc, Hilaire. *The Bad Child's Pop-Up Book of Beasts.* Illustrated by Wallace Tripp. New York: G. P. Putnam's Sons, 1982.

Berger, Barbara. *Grandfather Twilight.* New York: Philomel Books, 1984.

Bess, Clayton. *Tracks.* Boston: Houghton Mifflin, 1986.

Blos, Joan W. *Old Henry.* New York: William Morrow, 1987.

Blumenthal, Nancy. *Count-A-Saurus.* New York: Four Winds Press, 1989.

Bond, Michael. *A Bear Called Paddington.* New York: Dell, 1968.

Boynton, Sandra. *A Is for ANGRY.* New York: Workman Publishing, 1983.

Bradman, Tony. *Look Out, He's Behind You!* New York: Putnam, 1988.

Bradman, Tony, and Philippe Dupasquier. *The Sandal.* New York: Biking Kestrel, 1989.

Brandt, Keith. *Indian Crafts.* Mahwah, N.J.: Troll Associates, 1985; *Indian Homes.* Mahwah, N.J.: Troll Associates, 1985; *Planets and the Solar System.* Mahwah, N.J.: Troll Associates, 1985.

Bridwell, Norman. *Clifford: The Big Red Dog.* New York: Scholastic, 1985.

Brighton, Catherine. *Five Secrets in a Box.* New York: E. P. Dutton, 1987.

Brink, Carol Ryrie. *Caddie Woodlawn.* New York: Macmillan, 1973.

Brisson, Pat. *Kate Heads West.* New York: Bradbury Press, 1990.

Brown, Laurene Krasny, and Marc Brown. *Dinosaurs Divorce: A Guide for Changing Families.* Boston: Joy Street Books, 1986; *Dinosaurs Travel: A Guide for Families on the Go.* Boston: Joy Street Books, 1988; *Visiting the Art Museum.* New York: E. P. Dutton, 1986.

Brown, Marc. *Finger Rhymes.* New York: E. P. Dutton, 1980; *Play Rhymes.* New York: E. P. Dutton, 1987.

Brown, Marc, and Stephen Krensky. *Dinosaurs, Beware!* Boston: Joy Street Books, 1982.

Brown, Margaret Wise. *The City Noisy Book.* New York: Harper & Row, 1989; *David's Little Indian.* Birmingham, Ala.: Hopscotch Books, 1989; *The Dead Bird.* New York: Harper & Row, 1958; *Goodnight Moon.* New York: Harper & Row, 1947; *The Important Book.* New York: Harper & Row, 1949; *The Little Fireman.* New York: Harper & Row, 1952; *The Runaway Bunny.* New York: Harper & Row, 1970.

Bruxner, Mervyn. *Letters to a Musical Boy.* London: Oxford University Press, 1966.

Buscaglia, Leo. *The Fall of Freddie the Leaf.* New York: Charles B. Slack, 1982.

Butler, M. Christina. *Too Many Eggs: A Counting Book.* Boston: David R. Godine, 1988.

Butterfield, L. H., Marc Friedlander, and Mary-Jo Kline, eds. *The Book of Abigail and John: Selected Letters of the Adams Family, 1762-1784.* Cambridge, Mass.: Harvard University Press, 1975.

Butzow, Carol M., and John W. Butzow. *Science through Children's Literature.* Englewood, Colo.: Libraries Unlimited, 1989.

Campbell, Rod. *My Presents.* New York: Aladdin Books, 1989.

Carle, Eric. *The Grouchy Ladybug.* New York: Harcourt Brace Jovanovich, 1977; *The Honeybee and the Robber: A Moving Picture Book.* New York: Philomel Books, 1981; *A House for a Hermit Crab.* Saxonville, Mass.: Picture Book Studio, 1987; *The Mixed-Up Chameleon.* San Diego: Harper & Row, 1988; *1, 2, 3, to the Zoo.* New York: Philomel Books, 1982; *Papa, Please Get the Moon for Me.* Natik, Mass.: Picture Book Studio, 1986; *The Secret Birthday Message.* New York: Harper & Row, 1986; *The Tiny Seed.* Saxonville, Mass.: Picture Book Studio, 1987; *The Very Busy Spider.* New York: Philomel Books, 1984; *The Very Hungry Caterpillar.* New York: Philomel Books, 1981; *The Very Quiet Cricket.* New York: Philomel Books, 1990.

Carrick, Carol. *Big Old Bones: A Dinosaur Tale.* New York: Clarion Books, 1989; *Patrick's Dinosaurs.* New York: Clarion Books, 1983; *What Happened to Patrick's Dinosaurs?* New York: Clarion Books, 1986.

Carter, David A. *How Many Bugs in a Box?* New York: Simon & Schuster Books for Young Readers, 1988; *More Bugs in Boxes.* New York: Simon & Schuster Books for Young Readers, 1990; *Surprise Party.* New York: Grosset & Dunlap, 1990.

Cauley, Lorinda Bryan. *The Trouble with Tyrannosaurus Rex.* San Diego: Harcourt Brace Jovanovich, 1988.

Ciardi, John. *Fast and Slow: Poems for Advanced Children of Beginning Parents.* Boston: Houghton Mifflin, 1975.

Climo, Shirley. *The Egyptian Cinderella.* Illustrated by Ruth Heller. New York: Thomas Y. Crowell, 1989.

Colgin, Mary Lou, comp. *One Potato, Two Potato, Three Potato, Four: 165 Chants for Children.* Mt. Rainer, Md.: Gryphon House, 1982.

Conaway, Judith, and Renzo Barto. *More Science Secrets.* Mahwah, N.J.: Troll Associates, 1987.

Craig, Janet. *Amazing World of Spiders.* Mahwah, N.J.: Troll Associates, 1989.

cummings, e. e. *The Complete Poems, 1913-1962.* New York: Harcourt Brace Jovanovich, 1972.

Day, Alexandra. *Frank and Ernest.* New York: Scholastic, 1988.

de Beer, Hans. *Ahoy There, Little Polar Bear.* New York: North-South Books, 1988; *Little Polar Bear.* New York: North-South Books, 1987; *The Little Polar Bear Address Book.* New York: North-South Books, 1990; *The Little Polar Bear Birthday Book.* New York: North-South Books, 1990; *Little Polar Bear Finds a Friend.* New York: North-South Books, 1989.

de Paola, Tomie. *Now One Foot, Now the Other.* New York: G. P. Putnam's Sons, 1980.

de Regniers, Beatrice Schenk, ed. *Sing a Song of Popcorn.* New York: Scholastic, 1988.

de Rico, Ul. *The Rainbow Goblins.* New York: Warner Books, 1978.

De Vries, Leonard. *A Treasury of Illustrated Children's Books: Early Nineteenth-Century Classics from the Osborne Collection.* New York: Abbeville Press, 1989.

Ehlert, Lois. *Color Farm.* New York: J. P. Lippincott, 1990; *Color Zoo.* New York: J. P. Lippincott, 1989; *Eating the Alphabet.* San Diego: Harcourt Brace Jovanovich, 1989; *Feathers for Lunch.* New York: Harcourt Brace Jovanovich, 1990; *Fish Eyes: A Book You Can Count On.* San Diego: Harcourt Brace Jovanovich, 1990; *Growing Vegetable Soup.* New York: Harcourt Brace Jovanovich, 1987; *Planting a Rainbow.* New York: Harcourt Brace Jovanovich, 1988.

Elting, Mary, and Michael Folsom. *Q Is for Duck.* New York: Clarion Books, 1980.

Emberley, Rebecca. *Jungle Sounds.* Boston: Little, Brown, 1989.

Feelings, Muriel. *Jambo Means Hello: A Swahili Alphabet Book.* New York: Dial Books for Young Readers, 1974; *Moja Means One: A Swahili Counting Book.* New York: Dial Books for Young Readers, 1971.

Finch, Christopher. *The Art of Walt Disney.* New York: Harry N. Abrams, 1973.

Flack, Jerry D. *Inventing, Inventions, and Inventors.* Englewood, Colo.: Libraries Unlimited, 1989.

Flack, Marjorie. *Ask Mr. Bear.* New York: Aladdin Books, 1986.

Fleischman, Paul. *I Am Phoenix: Poems for Two Voices.* New York: Harper & Row, 1985; *Joyful Noise: Poems for Two Voices.* New York: Harper & Row, 1988.

Fox, Dan, arranger, and Claude Marks, commentary. *Go In and Out the Window.* New York: The Metropolitan Museum of Art/Henry Holt & Co., 1987.

Fox, Mem. *Hattie and the Fox.* New York: Bradbury Press, 1988.

Fraser, Antonia, ed. *Love Letters: An Illustrated Anthology.* Chicago: Contemporary Books, 1989.

Fraser, Betty. *First Things First: An Illustrated Collection of Sayings.* New York: Harper & Row, 1990.

Fritz, Jean. *Homesick: My Own Story.* New York: G. P. Putnam's Sons, 1984.

Gackenbach, Dick. *With Love from Gran.* New York: Clarion Books, 1989.

Gardner, Marjory, Heather Philpott, and Jane Tanner. *Time for a Rhyme.* Melbourne, Australia: Thomas Nelson Australia, 1989.

Gibbons, Gail. *The Pottery Place.* New York: Harcourt Brace Jovanovich, 1987.

Gordon, Karen Elizabeth. *The Well-Tempered Sentence: A Punctuation Handbook for the Innocent, the Eager, and the Doomed.* New Haven, Conn.: Ticknor & Fields, 1983.

Gray, Nigel. *A Balloon for Grandad.* New York: Orchard Books, 1988.

Greenaway, Kate. *A: Apple Pie: An Old Fashioned Alphabet Book.* London: Frederick Warne Activity Book, 1886.

Greenfield, Eloise. *Daydreamers.* New York: Dial Books for Young Readers, 1981.

Grifalconi, Ann. *Darkness and the Butterfly.* Boston: Little, Brown, 1987; *The Village of Round and Square Houses.* Boston: Little, Brown, 1986.

Griffin, Sandra Ure. *Earth Circles.* New York: Walker, 1989.

Gwynne, Fred. *A Chocolate Moose for Dinner.* New York: Simon & Schuster, 1976.

Handford, Martin. *Where's Waldo?* Boston: Little, Brown, 1987.

Copyright 1991 Teacher Ideas Press, a division of Libraries Unlimited, Inc., P.O. Box 3988, Englewood, CO 80155-3988

Hay, John. *Mama, Were You Ever Young?* San Diego: Green Tiger Press, 1989.
Hellen, Nancy. *Old MacDonald Had a Farm.* New York: Orchard Books, 1990.
Heller, Ruth. *Animals Born Alive and Well.* New York: G. P. Putnam's Sons, 1982; *A Cache of Jewels and Other Collective Nouns.* New York: G. P. Putnam's Sons, 1987; *Chickens Aren't the Only Ones.* New York: G. P. Putnam's Sons, 1981; *Kites Sail High: A Book about Verbs.* New York: Grosset & Dunlap, 1989; *Many Luscious Lollipops: A Book about Adjectives.* New York: Grosset & Dunlap, 1989; *Merry-Go-Round: A Book about Nouns.* New York: Grosset & Dunlap, 1990; *Plants That Never Ever Bloom.* New York: G. P. Putnam's Sons, 1984; *The Reason for a Flower.* New York: Grosset & Dunlap, 1983.
Hendrickson, Robert. *American Talk: The Words and Ways of American Dialects.* New York: Penguin Books, 1986.
Hennessy, B. G. *Eeney, Meeney, Miney, Mo.* New York: Viking, 1990.
Hernandez, Xavier, and Pilar Comes. *Barmi: A Mediterranean City through the Ages.* Boston: Houghton Mifflin, 1990.
Heuck, Sigrid. *Who Stole the Apples.* New York: Alfred A. Knopf, 1986.
Hilton, Lisa, and Sandra L. Kirkpatrick. *If Dinosaurs Were Alive Today.* Los Angeles: Price Stern Sloan, 1988.
Hine, Al, and John Alcorn. *A Letter to Anywhere.* New York: Harcourt Brace & World, 1965.
Hirst, Robin, and Sally Hirst. *My Place in Space.* New York: Orchard Books, 1988.
Hissey, Jane. *Old Bear.* New York: Philomel Books, 1986.
Hoban, Russell. *Egg Thoughts and Other Frances Songs.* New York: Harper & Row, 1972.
Hoban, Tana. *Look! Look! Look!* New York: Greenwillow Books, 1988.
Hobbs, Will. *Changes in Latitudes.* New York: Atheneum Children's Books, 1988.
Holder, Heidi, illus. *Crows: An Old Rhyme.* New York: Farrar, Straus & Giroux, 1987.
Hopkins, Lee Bennett. *Dinosaurs.* New York: Harcourt Brace Jovanovich, 1987.
Hubbard, Woodleigh. *C Is for Curious.* San Francisco: Chronicle Books, 1990.
Hughes, Patrick. *More on Oxymoron.* New York: Penguin Books, 1983.
Hunt, Cecil. *Word Origins: The Romance of Language.* New York: Philosophical Library, 1949.
Inkpen, Mike. *The Blue Balloon.* Boston: Little, Brown, 1989.
Irving, Jan. *Fanfares: Programs for Classrooms and Libraries.* Englewood, Colo.: Libraries Unlimited, 1990.
Irving, Jan, and Robin Currie. *Mudluscious: Stories and Activities Featuring Food for Preschool Children.* Littleton, Colo.: Libraries Unlimited, 1986.
Johnston, Tony. *Whale Song.* New York: G. P. Putnam's Sons, 1987.
Jonas, Ann. *The Trek.* New York: Mulberry Books, 1985.
Jones, Carol, illus. *Old MacDonald Had a Farm.* Boston: Houghton Mifflin, 1989; *This Old Man.* Boston: Houghton Mifflin, 1990.
Joslyn, Ruth. "Using Concrete Models to Teach Large Number Concepts," *Arithmetic Teacher* 38, no. 3 (November 1990): 6-9.
Joyce, William. *Dinosaur Bob and His Adventures with the Family Lazardo.* New York: Harper & Row, 1988.
Kempadoo, Manghanita. *Letters of Thanks: A Christmas Tale.* New York: Simon & Schuster, 1969.
Koci, Marta. *Sarah's Bear.* Natick, Mass.: Picture Book Studio, 1987.
Kowalczyk, Carolyn. *Purple Is Part of a Rainbow.* Chicago: Children's Press, 1985.
Kruise, Carol Sue. *Learning through Literature: Activities to Enhance Reading, Writing, and Thinking Skills.* Englewood, Colo.: Libraries Unlimited, 1990.
Lang, H. Jack, ed. *Letters in American History: Words to Remember.* Cleveland, Ohio: Harmony Books, 1982.
Latrobe, Kathy Howard, and Mildred Knight Laughlin. *Readers Theatre for Young Adults.* Englewood, Colo.: Libraries Unlimited, 1990.
Laughlin, Mildred Knight, and Kathy Howard Latrobe. *Readers Theatre for Children.* Englewood, Colo.: Libraries Unlimited, 1990.
Leedy, Loreen. *The Furry News: How to Make a Newspaper.* New York: Holiday House, 1990.
Lester, Helen. *It Wasn't My Fault.* Boston: Houghton Mifflin, 1985.
Levitt, Paul M., Douglas A. Burger, and Elissa S. Guralnick. *The Weighty Word Book.* Longmont, Colo.: Bookmakers Guild, 1985.
Lionni, Leo. *Little Blue and Little Yellow.* New York: Astor Book, 1959.
Lobel, Arnold. *The Book of Pigericks: Pig Limericks.* New York: Harper & Row, 1983.
Lyon, George Ella. *A B Cedar: An Alphabet of Trees.* New York: Orchard Books, 1989.
Macaulay, David. *The Way Things Work.* Boston: Houghton Mifflin, 1988.
MacDonald, Golden [Margaret Wise Brown]. *The Little Island.* New York: Doubleday, 1946.
MacLachlan, Patricia. *Sarah, Plain and Tall.* New York: Harper & Row, 1985.
Martin, Bill, Jr. *Brown Bear, Brown Bear, What Do You See?* New York: Henry Holt, 1983.
Martin, Bill, Jr., and John Archambault. *Barn Dance.* New York: Henry Holt, 1986; *Chicka Chicka Boom Boom.* New York: Simon & Schuster Books for Young Readers, 1989; *The Ghost-Eye Tree.* New York: Henry Holt, 1985; *Here Are My Hands.* New York: Henry Holt, 1985; *Knots on a Counting Rope.* New York: Henry Holt, 1987; *Listen to the Rain.* New York: Henry Holt, 1988; *Up and Down on the Merry-Go-Round.* New York: Henry Holt, 1985; *White Dynamite and the Curly Kidd.* New York: Henry Holt, 1986.
Mason, Laura. *A Book of Boxes.* New York: Simon & Schuster Books for Young Readers, 1989.
Mathis, Sharon Bell. *The Hundred Penny Box.* New York: Puffin Books, 1975.
Mayers, Florence Cassen. *ABC: The Wild West Buffalo Bill Historical Center, Cody, Wyoming.* New York: Harry N. Abrams, 1990.
McDermott, Gerald. *Anansi the Spider: A Tale from the Ashanti.* New York: Henry Holt, 1972.
McElmeel, Sharron. *An Author a Month (for Pennies).* Englewood, Colo.: Libraries Unlimited, 1988; *Bookpeople: A First Album.* Englewood, Colo.: Libraries Unlimited, 1990; *Bookpeople: A Second Album.* Englewood, Colo.: Libraries Unlimited, 1990.
McGuire, Leslie. *Nibbles Takes a Nibble.* New York: Merrimack Publishing, 1983.
McKee, David. *Elmer.* New York: Lothrop, Lee & Shepard Books, 1968.

McLenighan, Valjean. *One Whole Doughnut, One Doughnut Hole.* Chicago: Children's Press, 1982.
McMillan, Bruce, and Brett McMillan. *Puniddles.* Boston: Houghton Mifflin, 1982.
McPhail, David. *The Bear's Toothache.* Boston: Joy Street Books, 1988; *First Flight.* Boston: Little, Brown, 1987; *Fix-It.* New York: E. P. Dutton, 1984; *Snow Lion.* Boston: Parents, 1987.
Milne, A. A. *The House at Pooh Corner.* New York: E. P. Dutton, 1988; *Winnie the Pooh.* New York: Dutton, 1961, 1988.
Milton, Joyce. *Dinosaur Days.* New York: Random House, 1985.
Minarik, Else H. *Little Bear.* New York: Harper & Row, 1978.
Mitchell, Lucy Sprague. *Another Here and Now Story Book.* New York: E. P. Dutton, 1965.
Moerbeek, Kees, and Carla Dijs. *Hot Pursuit.* Los Angeles: Price Stern Sloan, 1987; *When the Wild Pirates Go Sailing.* Los Angeles: Price Stern Sloan, 1990.
Monjo, F. M. *Letters to Horseface: Being the Story of Wolfgang Amadeus Mozart's Journey to Italy, 1769-1770, When He Was a Boy of Fourteen.* New York: Viking Press, 1975.
Mosley, Francis. *The Dinosaur Eggs.* New York: Barron's, 1988.
Myers, Robert Manson, ed. *The Children of Pride.* New Haven, Conn.: Yale University Press, 1972.
Neumeier, Marty, and Byron Glaser. *Action Alphabet.* New York: Greenwillow Books, 1985.
Nixon, Joan L. *In the Face of Danger: The Orphan Train Quartet.* New York: Starfire, 1988.
Noble, Trinka Hakes. *The Day Jimmy's Boa Ate the Wash.* New York: Dial Books for Young Readers, 1980; *Jimmy's Boa and the Big Splash Birthday Bash.* New York: Dial Books for Young Readers, 1989.
Nolan, Dennis. *Dinosaur Dream.* New York: Macmillan, 1990.
Numeroff, Laura Joffe. *If You Give a Mouse a Cookie.* New York: Harper & Row, 1985.
Nygren, Tord. *The Red Thread.* Stockholm: Raben & Sjogren Books, 1987.
Offen, Hilda. *Little Miss Muffet.* New York: W. H. Smith, 1989.
O'Neill, Mary. *Hailstones and Halibut Bones: Adventures in Colors.* New York: Doubleday, 1973.
Pallotta, Jerry. *The Icky Bug Alphabet Book.* Watertown, Mass.: Charlesbridge, 1986.
Parish, Peggy. *Amelia Bedelia.* New York: Harper & Row, 1963.
Parker, Nancy Winslow, and Joan Richards Wright. *Bugs.* New York: Mulberry Books, 1987.
Parks, Brenda, and Judith Smith. *The Enormous Watermelon.* Crystal Lake, Ill.: Rigby, 1986 (reprinted 1989).
Peek, Merle. *Mary Wore Her Red Dress and Henry Wore His Green Sneakers.* New York: Clarion Books, 1985.
Pelham, David. *Worms Wiggle.* Illustrated by Michael Foreman. New York: Simon & Schuster, 1989.
Pellegrino, Virginia. *Listen to the Country.* Los Angeles: Price Stern Sloan, 1988.
Prelutsky, Jack. *Something BIG Has Been Here.* New York: Greenwillow Books, 1990.
Provensen, A., and M. Provensen. *Leonardo da Vinci.* New York: Viking Press, 1984.
Robinson, Elva. *Be Quiet, Go Slowly: A Science Predictable Storybook.* Allen, Tex.: DLM Teaching Resources, 1989.
Rylant, Cynthia. *Night in the Country.* New York: Bradbury Press, 1986.
Santrey, Laurence. *Discovering the Stars.* Mahwah, N.J.: Troll Associates, 1982.
Schwartz, David M. *How Much Is a Million?* New York: Lothrop, Lee & Shepard Books, 1989; *If You Made a Million.* Illustrated by Steven Kellogg. New York: Lothrop, Lee & Shepard Books, 1989.
Schwartz, Henry. *How I Captured a Dinosaur.* New York: Orchard Books, 1989.
Scruggs, Joe. *Deep in the Jungle* (cassette tape). Austin, Tex.: Educational Graphics Press, 1987.
Seeley, Laura L. *The Book of Shadowboxes: The Story of the ABC's.* Atlanta, Ga.: Peachtree Publishers, 1990.
Serfozo, Mary. *Who Said Red?* New York: Margaret K. McElderry Books, 1988.
Seymour, Peter. *Baby Dino's Busy Day.* Los Angeles: Price Stern Sloan, 1988; *What's in a Jungle?* Illustrated by David A. Carter. New York: Henry Holt, 1988.
Shapiro, Alan. *The House on Main Street.* New York: Simon & Schuster, 1989.
Sharmat, Marjorie Weinman. *I'm Terrific.* New York: Scholastic, 1977.
Sheppard, Jeff. *The Right Number of Elephants.* New York: Harper & Row, 1990.
Silverstein, Shel. *Where the Sidewalk Ends.* New York: Harper & Row, 1974.
Sneve, Virginia Driving Hawk, ed. *Dancing Teepees: Poems of American Indian Youth.* Illustrated by Stephen Gammell. New York: Holiday House, 1989.
Sohn, David. *Film: The Creative Eye.* Dayton, Ohio: Geo. A. Pflaum, 1970.
Stanley, Diane, and Peter Vennema. *Shaka: King of the Zulus.* New York: Morrow Junior Books, 1988.
Sterne, Noelle. *Tyrannosaurus Wrecks: A Book of Dinosaur Riddles.* New York: Harper & Row, 1979.
Tafuri, Nancy. *Junglewalk.* New York: Greenwillow Books, 1988.
Thayer, Jane. *Quiet on Account of Dinosaur.* New York: Mulberry Books, 1964.
Thurber, James. *Many Moons.* New York: Harcourt Brace Jovanovich, 1975.
Titherington, Jeanne. *Pumpkin Pumpkin.* New York: Greenwillow Books, 1986.
Turkle, Brinton. *Deep in the Forest.* New York: E. P. Dutton, 1976.
Van Allen, Roach. *Science Predictable Storybooks: A Teacher's Guide.* Allen, Tex.: DLM Teaching Resources, 1989; *When All the World's Asleep.* Allen, Tex.: DLM Teaching Resources, 1989.
Van Allsburg, Chris. *Ben's Dream.* Boston: Houghton Mifflin, 1982; *The Stranger.* Boston: Houghton Mifflin, 1986; *The Z Was Zapped.* Boston: Houghton Mifflin, 1987.
Van Buren, Abigail. *The Best of Dear Abby.* Kansas City, Mo.: Andrews & McMeel, 1989.

Vasari, Giorgio. *Lives of the Artists*. New York: Penguin, 1966.
Voight, Cynthia. *Dicey's Song*. New York: Atheneum Children's Books, 1982; *Homecoming*. New York: Atheneum Children's Books, 1981.
Waber, Bernard. *Ira Sleeps Over*. Boston: Houghton Mifflin, 1972.
Walsh, Ellen Stoll. *Mouse Paint*. New York: Harcourt Brace Jovanovich, 1989.
White, E. B. *Charlotte's Web*. New York: Harper & Row, 1989.
Whitman, Walt. *Complete Poetry and Selected Prose*. Boston: Rivers Edge Press, 1972.
Wilkinson, Marguerite. *Bluestone*. New York: Macmillan, 1920 (also in Johnson, Edna, ed. *Anthology of Children's Literature*. Boston: Houghton Mifflin, 1970).
Williams, Vera B., and Jennifer Williams. *Stringbean's Trip to the Shining Sea*. New York: Greenwillow Books, 1988.
Willis, Jeanne. *Earthlets as Explained by Professor Xargle*. New York: E. P. Dutton, 1988.
Wood, Audrey, and Don Wood. *Quick as a Cricket*. Singapore: Child's Play (International), 1982.
Wood, Don, and Audrey Wood. *The Little Mouse, the Red Ripe Strawberry, and the Big Hungry Bear*. Singapore: Child's Play (International), 1984.
Wright, Denise Anton. *One-Person Puppet Plays*. Englewood, Colo.: Libraries Unlimited, 1990.
Yolen, Jane. *Dinosaur Dances*. New York: G. P. Putnam's Sons, 1990; *Ring of Earth: A Child's Book of Seasons*. San Diego: Harcourt Brace Jovanovich, 1986.
Young, Ruth. *A Trip to Mars*. New York: Orchard Books, 1990.
Ziefert, Harriet, and Mavis Smith. *In a Scary Old House*. New York: Puffin Books, 1989.

Copyright 1991 Teacher Ideas Press, a division of Libraries Unlimited, Inc., P.O. Box 3988, Englewood, CO 80155-3988